Hill S
Wicklow

39 Easy Walks in the Dublin and Wicklow Mountains

David Herman

Shanksmare Publications

'Would you be so kind as to tell me which way I should go,' said Alice.
'That depends to a great extent on where you want to get to,' said the cat.
'I don't know exactly', said Alice.
'Then it doesn't matter which way you go either', said the cat.
'Alice in Wonderland' by Lewis Carroll

CONTENTS

Introduction

The Route Descriptions; Getting to the Mountains by Car; Getting to the Mountains by Bus; The Country Code; Rights of Way; Safety; A Few Route Selections; They're Your Mountains Too - Get Involved; Working Out Your Own Route.

* Route with Variation
† Route that is entirely different
from the 1994 edition of this book

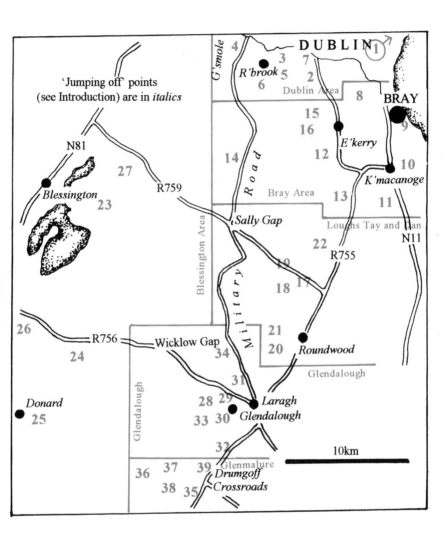

INTRODUCTION

This new edition of 'Hill Strollers Wicklow' contains most of the routes given in the previous version in 1994, plus some new ones and some modified routes. Specifically:

- 16 of the routes are the same or much the same as those in the 1994 version.
- 13 are substantially modified from that version.
- 10 are entirely different.

In choosing routes I have kept in mind the principles that informed previous editions. These are that the routes:

- Should avoid dense coniferous forest as far as possible, on the grounds that when you have seen one conifer you have seen them all.
- Should be looped rather than there-and-back.
- Should keep to tracks and paths to minimise navigation problems. Not that keeping to tracks and paths entirely eliminates such problems but they do tend to make errors less worrying when they occur.

It hardly needs saying that I have not been able to implement these principles throughout, especially the first two (though nearly all the routes keep to paths and tracks nearly all the way).

May I wish you a happy and rewarding time exploring the hills around Dublin!

THE ROUTE DESCRIPTIONS

The sketch maps: These are at a uniform scale, about 3cm to the kilometre (about 2 inches to the mile). Many of the maps have *not* got north to the top of the page. Instead, either the start of the route (the section where confidence is likely to be most shaky) or the most complicated section is oriented so that you can read this section from bottom to top, so that what is on the right on the map will also be right on the ground etc. This should make it easier to read the map in these difficult sections.

The symbols on the sketch maps are explained on the inside back cover.

Other Maps: There are a few maps that you might consider purchasing before you start to walk the routes:

You may find a *Dublin street map* essential even though I have tried to cover the difficult business of getting out of the city by car in the next section.

The area of all the routes is covered (after a fashion) on the half-inch to the mile *Ordnance Survey sheet 16*; though not much use on the walks, it may be useful in getting to the start once you are out of Dublin.

Ordnance Survey 1:50 000 sheet 56 (especially) and *sheet 50* (marginally) cover all the routes and how to get to the starts. On the walk itself they are useful in identifying peaks and other features off the route, something this modest book cannot do. They might also be essential in finding your way off the mountains if you go seriously astray. Neither map is accurate in its depiction of paths and tracks.

The National Parks and Wildlife Service's *Glendalough 1:25 000 map*, obtainable at a modest cost from the Visitor Centre in Glendalough or from their headquarters at 51 St Stephen's Green, Dublin 2, covers an excellent area for walks around Glendalough. It shows paths and tracks accurately.

Navigation: There's more about this in the section on 'Safety' below. For the moment note that easily recognised, though not necessarily prominent features which will give you confidence that you are on the correct route and/or that are important for navigation are printed in red in the text and on the maps.

Walking Speed: It is impossible to know exactly how long it will take a person to walk any route. The times given are based on 4km per hour on the flat, plus 500m of climbing per hour. To these are added estimates for difficult terrain (rocky ground, no path etc). Some time is subtracted on a similarly unscientific basis for abnormally easy terrain eg tarmac. All in all, this is not a superhumanly energetic pace but it does not allow for stops. Please do not assume that you can comfortably complete the routes in the times given. Instead, add whatever you think fit for all the extras.

Dogs: Most of the area covered by this book is sheep country and farmers have lost too many sheep to marauding dogs to allow them to take kindly to your 'playful' mutt's pursuits. Dogs may be taken on most routes as long as they are kept under strict control. Those which are particularly suitable or unsuitable are indicated in the route descriptions.

GETTING TO THE MOUNTAINS BY CAR

I must first apologise for assuming that you are travelling from Dublin to the mountains. However, most hill walkers do come from Dublin and it is the one place which most parts of the mountains are easiest accessed.

Getting to the mountains from Dublin is not simple, mainly because of inadequate sign-posting. The 'jumping-off point' method is used here. For each route first drive from Dublin to the appropriate jumping-off point (indicated in *italics* in the paragraph 'Getting There' in the route description). From there drive to the starting point as indicated in the same paragraph.

Here are the jumping-off points (the figures in brackets given after each represents miles from central Dublin):

Blessington (18): Drive through Harold's Cross, Terenure and Templeogue following signs for the N81.

Donard (31): Follow signs for the N81, turning left at the 'Old Tollhouse', about 11 miles south of Blessington.

Drumgoff crossroads (Glenmalure) (36): Drive to *Laragh* (see below), continue on the R755 for about 1 mile. Fork right (signposted Glenmalure) for Drumgoff crossroads, which is about 4½ miles further on.

Enniskerry (13): Follow signs for Ranelagh and Dundrum, then drive straight ahead.

Glenasmole (9): Follow signs for the N81 (see *Blessington* above) to turn left at the roundabout which leads onto the M50. (Note: there may be alterations to the road network here shortly.) Turn right at the nearby tee onto the R114 and continue straight ahead for 3.7 miles, turning left here into Glenasmole (unsignposted).

Glendalough (31), *Laragh* (30): Follow signs for the M11/N11 initially through Leeson Street and Donnybrook. Turn right onto the R755 at Kilmacanoge.

Rockbrook (6): Follow signs for Rathfarnham, pass Rathfarnham Castle (on left), turn right shortly after at the Yellow House pub (on right). Continue straight ahead for about 2½ miles to the village.

Roundwood (26): As for *Glendalough* above.

Sally Gap (17), *Military Road*: Drive initially through Harold's Cross and Terenure following signs for Rathfarnham, pass Rathfarnham Castle (on left), turn right shortly after at the Yellow House pub (on right). Turn right onto Scholarstown Road 1.2 miles from the pub and second left almost immediately onto Stocking Lane and continue straight ahead.

A Word of Caution to Travellers by Car: There have been many thefts in recent years from cars parked in mountain locations. It is therefore advisable never to leave valuables in unattended cars. Do *not* leave a note visible in your car indicating when you intend to arrive back.

GETTING TO THE MOUNTAINS BY BUS

The following Dublin Bus services (☎ 01-873 4222) may be useful.

For **Howth** note the 31 and 31B services (Howth is also served by DART).

For the north-west corner of the mountains note the 47 (**Tibradden**, infrequent), 47A (**Rockbrook**, fairly frequent), 47B (**Grange Road**, fairly frequent), 49A (**Bohernabreena**, fairly frequent though there is a poor Sunday service).

For **Barnacullia, Glencullen**, note the 44B service (infrequent).

For the north-east note the 44 (**Enniskerry**, frequent), 185 (**Shop River** (about 2.5km west of Enniskerry), fairly frequent) and the 145 (**Kilmacanoge,** fairly frequent).

For the west (N81) note the 65 to **Blessington** (frequent), **Ballymore Eustace** and **Ballyknockan** (both very infrequent).

The St Kevin's Bus (☎ 01-281 8119) service runs from St Stephen's Green in Dublin through **Kilmacanoge**, **Roundwood** and **Laragh** to **Glendalough**.

Reid's Buses (☎ 0404-67671) runs a regular service between **Wicklow town** and **Glendalough**.

There are two Irish Bus / Bus Eireann local services (ie buses which stop anywhere as long as it is safe) which might be useful for hill walkers. They are bus timetable 132 (very infrequent) which runs from Dublin along the **N81** on the west with a stop at **Annalecky Cross** near Donard, and timetable 133 (frequent) which runs along the **N11** (with diversions to villages) on the east.

There is only one Irish Bus / Bus Eireann express (ie limited stop) service which might be useful for hill walkers. It is given on bus timetable 5 with variations which traverse each side of the mountains from Dublin. That on the west stops at **Blessington** (pick-up only) and at **Annalecky Cross**. That on the east stops at **Bray** and **Ashford**.

THE COUNTRY CODE

The Country Code is really plain ordinary politeness applied in the countryside. In brief:

- Don't stand on fence wire; it may look the same afterwards but will have been irretrievably strained.
- Leave gates closed (or open) just as you found them. If you have to climb gates do so at the hinged end.
- Don't trample crops.
- Don't frighten or disturb animals; keep your dog under control.
- Don't light fires in or near forests.
- Don't widen paths or bypass zig-zags. Path erosion is a growing problem in the mountains and you can help by keeping well away from eroded paths or (preferably) walking along their centre, even if muddy.
- If in doubt ask the owner's permission before crossing his/her land. Respect his/her privacy, particularly round dwellings.
- Litter: don't, don't, don't. Whether biodegradable or not, inconspicuous or not. Though it might seem beyond the call of duty, conscientious walkers pick up litter thrown by others. Remember, the local authorities cannot remove it in remote areas and it cannot remove itself. It doesn't require much effort to pick it up and dispose of it properly.

RIGHTS OF WAY

Except in State forests, in the Wicklow Mountains National Park and on the Wicklow Way you have no absolute right to be anywhere in the mountains. Especially near Dublin, farmers are understandably worried by the frequent vandalism with which they are faced. It is hard for them to distinguish between polite walkers and destructive yobbos. If you are in doubt, ask the landowner if you may cross his/her land.

One would have thought that with the passing of the Occupiers' Liability Act 1995, which removes any remaining doubt that landowners have responsibility for accidents that occur on their land, that there would be a more relaxed attitude to walkers. Not so. The Act has resulted in unfriendly signs ending with the words UNAUTHORISED ENTRY IS PROHIBITED. However, the good news is that the representatives of the ICMSA, the organisation behind these signs, have declared that they are not intended to prevent access for walkers. So that's all right then - unless you are unused to our strange ways and do not realise that signs can mean the exact opposite of what they declare.

Given this unsatisfactory state of affairs it is prudent to interpret signs rather than simply obey them. The routes in this book do not knowingly lead you into areas in which confrontations are likely but it is impossible to know where disputes may flare in the future.

SAFETY

With few exceptions, there is a guide - a path, track, river or forest edge - for every inch of each of these walks. Nevertheless, if you are careless (or indeed, if I have been careless in my route descriptions) this still won't prevent your getting lost. For this reason it might be a good idea to carry a map and compass, even a simple one. Watch out carefully for the junctions and landmarks described in the text and shown on the sketch maps. Don't forget that features may have changed between the time I explored the routes (most of them in the summer of 1997) and the time you come to walk them. If features do not correspond to what is in the book, retrace your steps or continue cautiously ahead looking out for some feature which may help you pick up the route again. Do not press on regardless if you think something is seriously amiss.

If you are new to hill walking try some of the easier routes first. You will get some idea of which these are by reading the paragraph 'Difficulties' at the start of each route description.

Lastly and most importantly, cut the walk short if deteriorating weather warrants it.

A FEW ROUTE SELECTIONS

If you have only a limited time in the Dublin area, have a car and wish to get a *varied* selection of routes you might consider the following:

Bray Head (route 9), sea-cliffs and excellent views over the Irish Sea.

Lough Dan (routes 18 or 19), a wooded valley surrounded by some of the best mountains in Wicklow.

The Spink (route 30) for its splendid high-level views down into Glendalough.

The Fraughan Rock Glen (route 36), a remote and highly scenic narrow valley terminated by a cascade.

Ballydonnell Brook (route 27) or the Upper Dodder valley (route 4), a touch of the 'real' Wicklow (even though the latter route is in county Dublin), areas of bogland and gently rolling hills.

THEY'RE YOUR MOUNTAINS TOO – GET INVOLVED

Ireland is a country with a 'healthy disregard' for the law, and no wonder, since the law in too many instances is only for show and not for enforcement. The end result of all this as far as the environment is concerned is littering, dumping, car wrecks, 'temporary dwellings' that moulder away for decades, and all the rest that are obvious to anyone who wants to see.

I wish there were a simple solution to all this, but there isn't. The best you can do is to obey the law yourself and join one of the voluntary organisations which care about the environment. If you are in a walking club help its conservation group or suggest that one be formed if there isn't one. Lastly, its no great hardship to pick up a little litter as you walk. There will still be plenty for others behind you!

WORKING OUT YOUR OWN ROUTE

After you have done a few of the walks in this book you will no doubt want to plan and walk a route of your own. This is one of the joys of hill walking and if approached with reasonable caution, is not too difficult or dangerous.

The following pointers may be of help.

Buy a good map of the area in which you want to walk. Have a look at the maps available in the section above, but note that OS sheets 50 and 56 are unfortunately inaccurate in their depiction of tracks and, with a few exceptions do not attempt to show paths. In this context may I respectfully draw your attention to the modest volume '*This Way Up!*' also published by Shanksmare which depicts many tracks and paths which end in open country.

Choose an area from the map that you are at least a little familiar with, preferably by having walked somewhere thereabouts. Have a look at the introduction to each of the six sections given in this book to get an idea of the type of terrain you are likely to encounter. Starting points given in this book or in '*This Way Up!*' might be useful. Look for tracks that run into mountain areas, though these normally yield only there-and-back routes, or river banks which are navigationally safe and usually scenic though again, usually only there-and-backs. Be careful about climbing peaks that you do not know. It is easy to get to the top since you have the slope as a guide. On the way down you will have no such help and in bad visibility you might find that descents in any direction look equally familiar, or worse equally unfamiliar - a frightening prospect.

THE DUBLIN AREA

This area close to the city has no sense of remoteness and is not over-exciting. Except for route 1 the routes traverse a virtual plateau whose flanks rise from the suburbs of the city itself. All of the area is easily accessible by road and has a good bus service. Remember that this is the area where most vandalism and trespassing occurs and most landowners are wary of walkers, however well-intentioned, crossing their lands.

ROUTE 1: HOWTH HEAD

Easy tracks and paths through an area offering a good deal of variety but little feeling of remoteness. This variety encompasses the village of Howth, a sea cliff and steep sea-facing slopes, rough fields, a low but rugged summit and a tiny cliff-bound wood. A suitable area for dogs.

Getting There: By car, take the well signposted road to Howth and park near the harbour. DART and the 31 bus provide a good public service.

Difficulties: None.

Walking Time: 3 hours (distance 9km, climb about 300m) but can be reduced.

Route: ① Keep the sea on the left to walk beside the harbour and up Balscad-

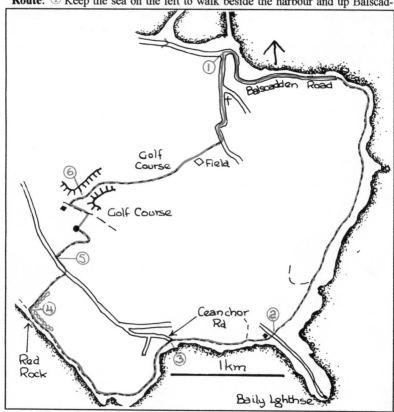

den Road. At its end take the Cliff Walk which continues onward and upward, with the sea far below. I find it hard to accept emotionally, whatever about logically, that this short section of the route is on a continuous curve to the right, so that first Ireland's Eye and Lambay beyond it are visible to the north, then the view encompasses the sea and finally one looks south to Bray Head and Wicklow Head far off to the south.

But back to mundane navigation. Ignoring minor paths continue on the Cliff Walk to pass by the base of the promontory crowned by the Bailey lighthouse. ② Cross the narrow tarmac road that ends at the lighthouse and on the other side take the path just to the left of the house 'Gale Point'. A few metres on, the path divides; take the right fork which passes through thick bushes below and close to houses on the right. Then turn left at the tee junction where a plaque at ground level indicates a right of way.

③ Further on the bollards just about visible on the right marking the end of Ceanchor Road are a distinctive landmark as well as a point where you can return by road to Howth in less than an hour (there's about 1½ hours to go on the route proper). If however you wish to continue, walk straight ahead on the Cliff Walk, which sweeps erratically up and down passing on the way fine rock pinnacles, secluded bathing places and impressive rocky cliffs.

The next landmark to look out for is a curious wall on the right paralleling the path, curious because its mortar consists mostly of sea-shells. ④ Where this wall swings abruptly inland at the tiny harbour of Red Rock, do likewise following a path initially directly and steeply uphill, though later the slope eases to cross rough fields before depositing the walker on the road.

Turn left here and after about 100m look out for a narrow path heading upward, marked at the time of writing by a post but no sign. ⑤ Take this path to reach the nearby rocky summit, from where the views are predictably excellent. On even a moderately clear day you should be able to see Slieve Donard in the Mournes 100km away to the north.

Descend north, still on the path, to reach a track running along the side of a golf course and turn left onto it for a few hundred metres, where there is a building on the left and more to the point, a right of way marked by a line of white stones across the golf course.

⑥ At the far side of the course, again on a path, you will enter a pleasant wood flanked by low, rocky cliffs. Towards the end of the wood, where the path tends to unravel into a maze of sub-paths, keep (another) golf course close on the left if you are in any doubt. About here head for goal posts and when you reach the associated pitch turn left to walk along the near goal line (hope they haven't changed the layout of the pitch by the time you arrive!). Beyond it continue straight ahead to find a narrow path which ends on the road. Turn left and follow it all the way down to the village and the harbour.

ROUTE 2: FAIRY CASTLE

One of the walks nearest to the city. Though this is hardly a recommendation, this walk packs in a lot of variety, none of it very exciting: heathery uplands, some forestry and three summits (or rather modestly swelling high points). Given its unfavourable location, as good a walk as can be expected.

Getting There: By car, drive to Lamb Doyle's restaurant on Blackglen Road and take the road on its right (Woodside Road). Drive for one mile to the Blue Light pub in the village of Barnacullia. Park near the pub. **By bus**, take the 44B to Barnacullia (infrequent) or the 44 to Lamb Doyle's.

Difficulties: A good deal of rough ground underfoot. Towards the end of the walk, with a wealth of paths and tracks to confuse, navigation is quite difficult. (I said in the previous edition of this book that navigation was 'generally easy'. Maybe so, but on mature reflection I now realise that the stretches not covered by that 'generally' are far from easy.)

Walking Time: 2¼ hours (distance 7km, climb 340m). The walking time for the easy variation is 1½ hours (distance 4km, climb 250m).

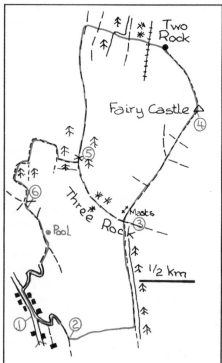

Route: ① Walk a little back towards Dublin, taking the first road on the left steeply uphill (signposted 'cul de sac'). Ignore a driveway on the right to take the track through quarry workings and so find yourself on a grassy track running roughly north and giving fine views of the city.

Tempting though it is to keep on this track it cannot be followed for more than a few minutes (if that), because the idea now is to reach the line of trees that climb the northern slopes of Three Rock.

② This means that a path has to be found on the left heading uphill. Paths there are aplenty, wandering aimlessly among the grass, bracken and worst of all, gorse which clothe these slopes, but to pick one that will reach the forest boundary is beyond my descriptive powers.

So, it's a question of trial and error, and no doubt you will at length find yourself at the clear path that runs by the side of the forest. Take it all the way to near the masts on the summit of Three Rock. Here you will have to make a decision whether to take the main route or the easy variation.

③ If you want to do the main route, follow the clear track to the right of the masts and climbing directly uphill towards Fairy Castle. Fork right onto a muddy path at the one decision point (there's also a track heading off on the level here which simply couldn't be the correct way) and climb directly to the cairn and trig pillar marking the top. A fine viewpoint and worth the effort, with wide views over Glencullen and beyond.

④ From Fairy Castle take the path to a heap of boulders near the summit of Two Rock nearby, heading towards the cone of Big Sugar Loaf if you have any doubt about direction. This heap does not seem to be one of the Rocks of Two Rock: these two tors lie a little further on over a decrepit fence. Walk to the nearer of them and then continue directly away from the fence to reach a track near a forest corner. At this corner take a rough firebreak downhill, forest on the right at first and then on both sides. Cross one narrow forest track to turn left onto the next. ⑤ Just after a forest bar, the point where the easy variation rejoins the main route turn right down a path (left of course for the easy variation). From here on to near the finish watch your navigation, as mistakes (not life-threatening ones) are possible.

This path traverses a short stretch with mature forest on the right and not quite so mature forest on the left. Turn right at the nearby tee and follow it round two right-angle bends to the left (you will glimpse the end of a wide forest track off to the right at the second). The path then takes you through a region of gorse, scattered forest and overgrown fields. Where it plunges straight into forest leave it to take a minor path on the right that skirts this forest.

A few minutes later you will arrive at a cross tracks (or cross paths) with the quarries of Barnacullia ahead a few hundred metres away. Don't continue straight ahead here as, if you were to, all would end in tears in high vegetation and private property. ⑥ Instead, turn left into forest, fork immediately right and so gain a nearby forest track, a wide and clear one.

Navigational problems are now at length behind. Turn right to follow this track past a deep pool on the left, fork right where the left is obviously going to terminate at nearby masts and wend your way down on a gradually improving path, then track, then narrow road to the village. Turn left on the main road for the nearby start.

Easy Variation: Turn left onto the gravel track on the summit of Three Rock and follow it between the tors until you see the forest bar ahead. ⑤ Take the path on the left just before it and continue the commentary for the main route above.

ROUTE 3: KILMASHOGUE

Though so close to the city, this is a surprisingly pleasant and unspoilt walk, taking in good views of the city and beyond (of course) and a quiet and placid valley (hardly expected). Ideal as a short walk on a summer's evening.

Getting There: By car, drive along College Road, turn off on the side opposite the wall of Marley Park onto Tibradden Road and fork left immediately. Park in Kilmashogue carpark on the left 0.7 miles from the fork. **By bus**, take route 47 to its terminus near the lower end of Kilmashogue Lane. The terminus of route

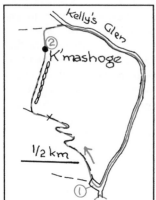

47B is over 2km from the start and the frequent route 16 is yet farther off but adds a pleasant walk through Marlay Park.

Difficulties: One short pathless stretch, otherwise track or tarmac underfoot and easy navigationally. There is the prospect of unfriendly notices and fencing, which you will have to use your judgement to interpret.

Walking Time: 1¼ hours (distance 3.5km, climb 240m).

Route: ① From the carpark take the track to the right of the waymarked Wicklow Way. The track climbs steeply through a mixture of mature and clear-felled forest, from which it emerges at an iron gate. Walk a few more metres to rough stone posts and here turn right and climb following a path and earthbank to a heap of stones. From here it is only a few metres to the summit cairn, located on a heathery plateau.

② Don't continue on the path from the summit. Instead walk directly onward aiming roughly for a vee of forest spilling over the hillside to the south. This will take you to a track (or if you should meet a firebreak fronting a fence and young trees instead, walk left to this track). Turn right onto the track to meet nearby tarmac. This takes you along the side of the pleasant Kelly's Glen, farmland and mountain off to the left, rough grazing land on the right, with the occasional tidy house on either side. Kilmashogue carpark is about 1km away.

ROUTE 4: THE UPPER DODDER VALLEY

A walk of contrasting halves: an old, pleasant track rising through a wide expanse of bogland gives easy walking, followed by some tough walking along a deep-set river, with views confined within the narrow vee of the steeply rising banks. A walk with a surprisingly remote air, though so close to Dublin.

Getting There: Turn left into *Glenasmole*, then drive straight ahead for 2.8 miles to a hairpin bend at the head of the valley. The one point where you might have doubts about the way is close to the hairpin bend where you take the right option. Parking is restricted at this bend, so if there are more than say, two cars in the party it might be prudent to look out for considerate parking along the road close to it.

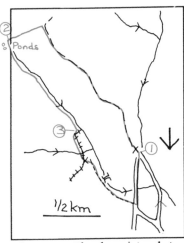

Difficulties: The initial track presents no difficulties, but the descent to the river bank and (especially) the first stage of the walk along the river involves walking through high vegetation and across steep slopes. If you can't bear bracken, avoid this section of the route in high summer.

Walking Time: 1¾ hours (distance 5.5km, climb 220m), with the difficult walking in the second half of the route compensated by easy walking in the first.

Route: ① Cross the gate at the hairpin bend and climb gently on the track beyond it. This is a lovely stretch of track, fine trees on the left and fields sloping down to the Cot Brook on the right. Soon however the route settles down into what will become its pattern for some time: on the left and near at hand the cleft formed by the deep-set Dodder; on the right and ahead bogland sweeping up to gently rolling mountains, of which the most distinguished is Kippure and that only because of its mighty TV masts.

After maybe a half-hour's steady walking, mostly uphill though you are now on the level, you should come to two large (tens of metres across) circular ponds on the left. ② The idea at about this second pond is to get to the deep cleft of the Dodder, reached in only a few minutes by walking north-east directly away from the left side of the track. (An aside: you can walk onward towards Kippure, but the track is muddier and the scenery not improved by the remains of cars etc, which some persons have taken the trouble to dump hereabouts.)

Having reached the *top* of the river bank you will note that there is a steep drop to the river itself and a precarious walk downstream alongside it. You can lessen the steep drop by wandering upstream and descending further up; this stroll (maybe stroll isn't quite the word for what might turn out to be a struggle through high heather) also gives excellent views down to the river.

When you do reach the river, cross it and walk downstream, where there is a not very useful intermittent path. This is a delightful stretch and a great contrast to the outward journey. Your world is confined to the steep vee of the banks with the exuberant Dodder chuckling its way along its bottom and with further on the prospect of some lovely old deciduous trees on the other bank.

Approaching the valley floor and the first signs of civilisation you will have to pay a little attention to navigation. The basic idea is to keep the Dodder, the stream you have been walking along, within reach on the left. ③ When you meet a fence, keep it on the left, then ford a narrow tributary of the Dodder. Next cross a gate, and with the Dodder now close at hand, pass (do not cross) a footbridge on the left. At this point you are on a clear track with the road close at hand. Turn left onto it for the nearby start.

ROUTE 5: TIBRADDEN

Close to the city and offering views over it as well as over much of the Dublin mountains, which unfortunately are rather gently rounded. Truth to tell, the route has one only slowly modifying view on the outward leg and a quite different but also only slowly modifying one on the return. A good area for an undemanding walk on a summer evening. This route can easily be combined with route 6.

Getting There: By car to *Rockbrook* village. Continue upward for a mile or so to turn left off the main road and park shortly in the large forest carpark on the left (Pine Forest). It's hardly worth doing this walk using the **bus** (route 47A to Rockbrook) but if you combine this walk with route 6 it might make sense. The walk up from Rockbrook is mostly uphill but pleasant. There is a short-cut path to the carpark which will reduce the road walk.

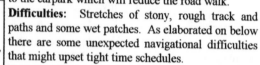

Difficulties: Stretches of stony, rough track and paths and some wet patches. As elaborated on below there are some unexpected navigational difficulties that might upset tight time schedules.

Walking Time: 1¾ hours (distance 6.5km, climb 180m), but this may be shortened as described below.

Route: To avoid navigational errors at the start, it might be just as well to follow the initial directions carefully. Note also that the distinction between 'track' and 'path', usually fairly clear, is difficult in this area, so you might well consider my 'tracks' to be your 'paths' and visa versa.

① Cross the bar at the end of the carpark, and take the track beyond. This leads shortly to an unforested area with fine views over the city and a wooded, agricultural landscape nearer at hand. At the tee turn right and left at the first track, a narrow one to start and certainly a path after only a few metres. After only a minute or so, and now you are on level ground, turn off to the right onto a narrow path through dense trees.

The path ends at a junction of forest tracks, where you continue straight ahead, so reaching a timber bar, a good reassurance point. ② Turn left at this bar to follow a track generally uphill. Fork right at the one point where a decision has to be made. (The narrow left fork alongside the fence is the return route: you might like to inspect it if you have doubts about walking over rough ground.)

Navigational problems are now over for a while and you can enjoy long views over Glencullen and the hills beyond. Walk by a passage grave on the right; at about the tor just beyond it you may decide to turn back, since the track ahead is likely to be wet and the views change only slowly, though they are quite good. If however you opt for the main route continue on what is now indisputably a path into low forest. ③ At the Wicklow Way post turn left onto what might uncharitably be described as a track crossed by mighty speed ramps, someone's idea of an 'improvement'.

Luckily, you have only to endure a few hundred metres on this crude gouging, because at the next waymark you turn left off the Way into scattered trees, forking left shortly onto a stony path rather than taking a vague track between fences. This path take you above the fields of Kelly's Glen, with Kilmashogue Mountain beyond. It's a pretty rough path, so watch your step.

At length this path joins a track, the one you were on previously. ④ Take it back to the timber bar, but this time go straight ahead steeply downhill on a path and so meet the end of a track. Turn right here (there's no other option) and walk a few metres to a junction. Turn left here and left again onto the first track, the one you started on, with the carpark only a few minutes away.

ROUTE 6: CRUAGH WOOD

A short and navigationally simple walk on tracks through State forest. Some (only some) of this forest consists of saplings or is mature and well-scattered, so giving good views over the city and far beyond. A good area for dogs.

Getting There: By car to *Rockbrook*. Continue upward on the main road for a further 2 miles to park on the left in Cruagh Wood carpark. **By bus** take the 47A to Rockbrook and walk to the start. A variation for travellers by bus is given below or, to make the journey worthwhile, you might like to combine this route with route 5.

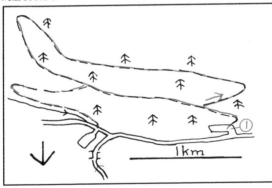

Difficulties: None.
Walking Time: 1 hour (distance 4km, climb 120m).
Route: ① From the carpark take the one and only track, turn first right off it and follow this track first gently uphill, and then round a hairpin bend and gently downhill.

Ignore a track on the right to walk directly back to the carpark.

If you have come by bus you might turn right onto the track met on the homeward leg. This takes you down to tarmac close to Pine Forest carpark, from where you can walk route 5. Alternatively you can continue straight ahead on tarmac and turn right onto the nearby main road to end up again in Rockbrook.

ROUTE 7: TICKNOCK

Though short, quite a varied route, though the views of the city and the coast are nowhere more than moderate. The whole area is degraded by big city super-structure (eg masts, roads) and carelessness (eg litter). A good area for dogs.

Getting There: With Lamb Doyle's pub on the left drive along Blackglen Road to turn first left onto Ticknock Road (this is one of several routes that are obvious from a street map). Drive uphill for 1.0 miles, turn left into forest. Drive uphill for 0.4 miles and park at a point where numerous tracks and paths diverge on the right. (Note: at the end of the walk you can drive downhill to reach the

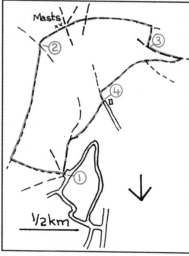

public road.) **By bus** take the 48A or the 47B to within 2km of the start; the 44B comes closest (within about 1.5km) but is infrequent.

Difficulties: The paths and tracks of this route form a confusing maze so that attention to the navigational details given might be prudent. However there are always plenty of people around, though whether they will know any more about their whereabouts than you is problematical.

Walking Time: 1¼ hours (distance 3.5km, climb 140m).

Route: ① Facing the direction where the tracks diverge take the path to the right of the barred track, that is the second option from the left. After a short stretch through forest, turn right to follow the forest edge, where good seaward views may alleviate the upwards toil.

At the gravel road near the mast-adorned top of Three Rock, you will see on its far side the prominent straight track climbing to Fairy Castle. ② Head towards this track, pass two masts close on the left and then take the second right of four radiating tracks. At the cross tracks just beyond continue straight ahead, thus keeping roughly on the level on a track that is gradually narrowing to path status. From around here you will see lower down on the right a tiny valley containing a disused rifle range, and beyond it the entire city.

Turn first right (you can't go ahead as the onward path ends after a few metres) and walk down to a track. ③ Turn left here and after about 5 minutes take the first narrow path running sharply back to the right (at this junction you will see a Wicklow Way marker just ahead). Continue straight ahead on it, rather than take any of several minor turns on the left. At its end, turn left onto a wider path to reach an old barn. ④ Turn right here, so taking the track to the right of a partly tarmac road. Walk straight ahead to a tee and turn left. Continue straight ahead steadily downhill to reach the start.

THE BRAY AREA

Small rocky hills close to the sea giving short but energetic walks (routes 8-11) with pleasant valleys inland giving walks on generally gentler terrain (routes 12-16), but not much sense of remoteness anywhere (except perhaps on parts of routes 12 and 13). Generally a good bus and train service. There is a 'bird's eye view of part of this area on page 29.

ROUTE 8: CARRICKGOLLOGAN

More familiarly known as 'Katty Gallagher', this hill rises to a modest 276m, but nonetheless commands views over quite an area of varied country and seascape. Except for the steep descent from the summit, the walk is along tracks and paths through gentle terrain.

Getting There: Take the road towards *Enniskerry*, pass through Kilternan, ignore the turn for Ballycorus Road on the left and take the next turn on this side

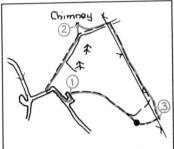

(there is a post-box at the junction). Drive onwards to the forest entrance on the right, turn left up a narrow road here and park in nearby Carrickgollogan forest carpark on the left. By 44 or 63 **bus** to Kiltiernan thus leaving a pleasant walk of over 2km each way to the start proper.

Difficulties: None.

Walking Time: ¾ hour (distance 3km, climb 80m).

Route: ① Retrace steps downhill from the carpark to turn right shortly onto a rough track directly under power lines. Take it towards and by the side of a nearby forest, beyond which walk to the old lead mine chimney. At 25m high, the chimney is an elegant edifice of granite blocks.

② Return to the nearest forest edge and turn left to head slightly downhill. At the electricity lines turn right to walk through a wide gap in the forest to head directly towards the summit of Carrickgollogan, so ignoring various tracks heading in other directions.

Do not follow the track where it swings right at the foot of the summit mound; instead follow the electricity lines uphill for a few more minutes until the ground starts to drop steeply. ③ At this point climb steeply to the right on a rough path to the summit itself. The view from the stony top is excellent, with the Sugar Loafs, Howth, Killiney and Bray Heads near at hand, plus much of Dublin's sprawling suburbs and a wide area of the north-east of the Wicklow mountains.

If you face directly towards the lead mine chimney from the summit you will see the next target: a track bounded by thick forest on the left only a few hundred metres away. Head directly down the steep slope towards it, and where the ground shortly levels off traverse a narrow stretch of forest with paths going every which way to gain it. Follow this track to reach the nearby carpark.

ROUTE 9: BRAY HEAD

A well-trodden, unfortunately littered route from Bray leads to excellent views far and near and to a surprisingly remote-seeming plateau bounded by the several rocky hillocks on the northern and southern tops of Bray Head. The return is along the Cliff Walk, which borders a coast of rocky outcrops under relentless assault from the ocean. Easy, varied walking and a good area for dogs.

Getting There: Drive to Strand Road Bray (follow the signs for the seafront), turn right near its southern end onto Putland Road, take the second left onto Edward Road and continue straight ahead to the carpark. If travelling by public transport walk along the seafront to take the Cliff Walk over the railway bridge and shortly after turn right up a path heading directly towards the Cross.

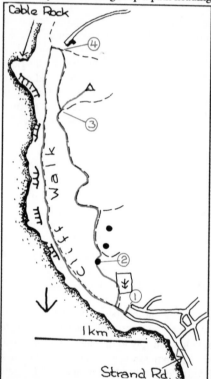

Difficulties: Some steep ground, otherwise easy.

Walking Time: 2 hours (distance 6km, climb 250m).

Route: ① Walk down the path at the end of the carpark to reach the nearby Cliff Walk. Turn right and right again shortly so facing the Cross crowning the north top of Bray Head and the first target. Climb steeply by an old plantation and then clamber over rocks to reach the Cross itself.

② From the Cross take the track running south - it's clearly visible from the Cross traversing a rough plateau. It's all quite a contrast to bustling Bray: a placid world with a great expanse of sea (and maybe a few of the Welsh peaks) off to the east and the bulk of the Wicklow mountains to the west.

Continue as far as a decrepit fence rounding a rocky knoll on the left and within sight of the trig pillar on the southern top of the Head. At this point you should also be able to see a small grassy promontory, Cable Rock, reaching seaward, with partly submerged rocks beyond it. This is of interest because about there you will meet the Cliff Walk and the return leg of the walk. ③ But before that cross the fence and walk to the trig pillar (240m) from where the views, especially those to the south towards Greystones and Wicklow Head beyond it are excellent.

That done, retrace your steps to the point where you crossed the fence and take the rough path downwards towards a group of buildings. ④ At these buildings turn left, still on a path, and walk down to the Cliff Walk, again turning left.

A word about the stretch from here back to Bray. It is, especially at first, a lovely walk. On one side: cliffs, the home to raucous sea-birds; far below the occasional stony beach edged by rocks; the single-line railway, its abandoned tunnels actually accentuating its remoteness. On both sides a wealth of flowers in the spring on the grassy slopes and between the ancient grey rocks

There is no alternative to the path along here so no need for navigational details. After 2km or so you will recognise the initial path and turn left up the narrow steps to reach the carpark.

ROUTE 10: LITTLE SUGAR LOAF

Little Sugar Loaf (342m), situated between the striking cone of Big Sugar Loaf and the bold promontory of Bray Head, is a delightful mountain, a line of rocky hummocks, though much of its vegetation was destroyed by fire in 1995. The eastern side is completely off limits (understandable, given the vandalism hereabouts) so this walk traverses the summit ridge from the western side.

Getting There: By car drive to *Kilmacanoge*, pass the turn for Glendalough and immediately after look out for a narrow road on the left (there is a house called 'Old Post Office' here which you should keep on the left). Drive a further 0.8

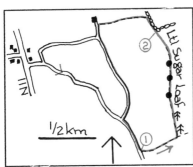

miles along the road to park on waste ground on the left. **By bus** take Dublin Bus route 145, Irish Bus table 133 or St Kevin's Bus to the village. You will see from the sketch map how to get directly back.

Difficulties: Some steep, stony ground.

Walking Time: 1¼ hours (distance 3.5km, climb 200 m).

Route: ① From the waste ground take the clear track heading to the south of the mountain. When barred by a line of old pines and an unfriendly sign turn left and climb over rocky ground directly to the first top. Along here you may be lucky enough to see the mountains of Wales; if not the wide views along the coast and to nearby Bray may be some consolation.

After the third hummock there is a rocky descent before the ground levels again at a corner of a stone wall. ② Here continue straight ahead down another short but steep stretch, at the bottom of which you should turn left onto a path heading just to the left of a nearby house, the only one around. Near the house turn left again onto a grassy track, and simply continue straight ahead on tracks and later a road right back to the start.

ROUTE 11: BIG SUGAR LOAF

Great Sugar Loaf (501m), known to its intimates as Big Sugar Loaf, is not a mountain of subtlety, being a classical cone without hidden valleys or subsidiary tops. All this blandness makes a direct assault easy and boring. This alternative runs partly above agricultural land and partly on the slopes of Sugar Loaf, unfortunately now a black, rocky desert after disastrous fires in 1995, though the wide views from the summit are unimpaired.

Getting There: By car to *Kilmacanoge*. Dublin Bus route 145, Irish Bus table 133 and St Kevin's Bus serve the village.

Difficulties: I have to confess to getting lost on the start of this route ... using a guidebook ... my own. However, mistakes should not be hazardous and after the initial stretch detailed directions can be dispensed with for some time. There is a little wet ground at the start.

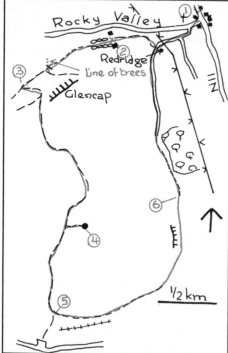

Walking Time: 3 hours (distance 8km, climb 440m) for the main route, 2½ hours (distance 5.5km, climb 440m) for the variation, which allows some time for the steep descent from the summit.

Route: ① From the village take the Glendalough road for a few metres, turning left onto the narrow road opposite the church. Continue straight ahead where the main road swings left. At the house 'Redridge' on the left, turn right onto a track. Ignoring side turnings - unhappy phrase - continue past or onto a narrow concrete road (it depends on your exact route) to reach a gate wedged between two houses that fronts a narrow lane bordered by stone walls.

(An aside: The reason for the cautionary phrase in the last paragraph is that it is hard to know which are side turnings and which is the main track. However, the narrow concrete road and the gate are unmistakable landmarks. The same applies to the line of trees mentioned in the paragraph after next.)

② Walk to the end of the lane and beyond it keep to any path (there are several crossing and diverting) keeping close to Rocky Valley on the right and further away from the cliffs and scree slopes of Glencap off to the left. (Please disabuse yourself of the comforting notion that the high point of Glencap is the summit of Big Sugar Loaf. It isn't, not by a long chalk.)

It is along here, assuming that you are heading even roughly in the correct direction, that you will see the line of trees running roughly at right angles to your path. Head for near the right end and you will find yourself on a track, which is still heading roughly parallel to the line of the Glencap cliffs. Shortly pass a track coming in from the left. ③ A few metres further on turn left acutely back up a grassy track.

After a few minutes on this track you will espy the summit of Sugar Loaf ahead. Now at least you have a clear view of your target and you can get there any way you like. However if you keep to the track (or main path) it will take you on a gentle slope round to the eastern side of the summit thus giving good views of Little Sugar Loaf. You will finally have to leave this track to climb a steep eroded path to the summit, of course an excellent viewpoint.

④ This is the point to decide whether to return directly to the start (see below) or to do the somewhat longer main route. If the latter, it may be no harm to get the general drift of the return from the summit, much of which can be seen from here. The idea is to head for the carpark on Calary Plateau to the south and before you get there to veer left so as to keep fields on the right, and then to head roughly parallel to the main road, the N11.

Retrace your steps down the eroded path and at the nearby main track turn left and head for the carpark. ⑤ Near it veer left away from it to reach a path beside a fence. Follow this path, so keeping fields on the right *for a while*.

From here back to the start I could invest many words in describing the route and you would be still none the wiser, since this is an area of paths and tracks running every which way. Suffice to give you two pointers. Firstly, don't climb; keep on the level or gently downhill all the way, so working your way round until you are parallel to the huge electricity pylons on the right and a few hundred metres from them. Secondly, as you advance watch out for a delightful wood tucked into low ground on the right. ⑥ Head towards it so as to reach it about half way along its length. If you haven't picked it up already, you will pick up a path along its side. This ends in tarmac, from where there is a straight walk onward into the village.

Short Variation: From the top of Sugar Loaf it is of course possible to return directly to the start. To do this head north-east (ie towards the central hummock of Little Sugar Loaf) over steep, initially rocky ground where the occasional snatch of path may be of some help. On your descent you should come across a deep gully on your left and if you follow this you will come to the wood mentioned above. Turn left here for the village.

Note

At first glance Big Sugar Loaf looks as if it is an extinct volcano. It isn't. It is composed of sandstone, the same type of rock displayed on Howth Head, Bray Head and indeed Little Sugar Loaf. You will see from the summit how different the craggy profiles of these mountains are to the bulk of the Wicklow mountains to the west. These are composed of granite which weathers into gently rounded shapes.

ROUTE 12: MAULIN AND CRONE WOOD

An increasingly dull forest walk ends high above the wooded bowl of the magnificent Deer Park with the silver stream of Powerscourt Waterfall ahead. The return is via the summit of Maulin (570m) which, because of its location at the edge of the range, gives marvellous wide views, and indeed marvellous near views towards the rocky cliffs of the Raven's Glen.

Getting There: Drive to *Enniskerry*. Take the road south, signposted Roundwood, turn right after 2.1 miles towards Glencree. Park in Crone carpark on the left 2.4 miles from this right turn.

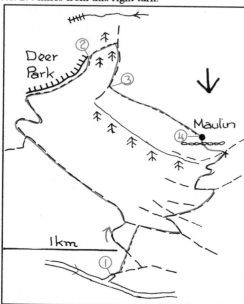

Difficulties: Some muddy stretches of path. Although you are unlikely to go wrong, a map and compass might be reassuring just in case.

Walking Time: 2¾ hours (distance 7km, climb 420m).

Route: ① Take the forest track from the carpark, turning left almost immediately onto a path. Walk this to the first track and turn left here to walk as far as a waymark, where you turn left to follow the Wicklow Way. As you advance, the forest, which initially allowed glimpses of field and gorse, presses ever closer, resulting in an all-encompassing Stygian gloom. When all seems lost, darkness is suddenly put to flight and the persevering walker emerges into the light. The scene here, viewed from the path you will walk high above the Deer Park modifies only slowly for the next 1km or so but is one worth savouring. The sylvan Park at your feet, Powerscourt Waterfall plunging over the encircling cliffs and the massive bulk of Djouce behind it. A memorable sight!

② Eventually you enter forest and, still following the Wicklow Way markers shortly emerge from it at a tumbled wall with Glensoulan down on the left and more to the point, the shoulder of Maulin up on the right. The idea now is to climb Maulin. Turn right uphill to follow a path along the forest edge. ③ When you reach the crest of the hill, turn left to follow a clear path to the summit. Clear and eroded, in fact, so do not widen it by walking on its edges.

There is cairn on the summit of Maulin so it's difficult to miss it (but not impossible). This is a marvellous viewpoint with the rocks on the summit of Djouce clearly visible to the south, the Tonduffs to the west, the valley of Glencree to the north and maybe even the rim of the corrie cut into Mullaghcleevaun away to the south-west.

④ From the cairn itself look north where you will see a nearby section of wall. Aim downhill just to the left of this section and as you do so watch out for a sturdy gate at the left of a straggly line of trees. This is your descent point but before crossing this gate it is worthwhile taking the level track onward to view the full majesty of the crags and waterfall of the Raven's Glen.

Back to the gate. As you will see from the sketch map there are several junctions from here to the carpark but you have to remember only two points: at every junction take the downward track and where there is still doubt take the main one. You will eventually come to a Wicklow Way signpost, where you turn left down a narrow path to reach the nearby carpark.

ROUTE 13: DJOUCE WOODS AND GLENSOULAN

A steady ascent with only slowly modifying views ends high on the shoulder of lofty Djouce and is followed by a stroll, though not an easy one, in the narrow, remote valley of Glensoulan. The return is mostly through forest.

Getting There: Car only. Drive through *Enniskerry*, taking the road south here, signposted Glendalough and Roundwood. Continue to follow signs for Roundwood for about 4½ miles, passing two forest carparks on the right, both signposted Djouce Woods. Park in the third carpark.

Difficulties: The walk along Glensoulan is on an intermittent, usually wet path, though this section may easily be omitted. Otherwise easy tracks and no serious navigation.

Walking Time: 2½ hours (distance 8km, climb 280m).

Route: ① From the carpark take the path (it's at the far end from the entrance), walk downhill, shortly branch left off it onto a minor path and so cross a narrow stream. On the right here you can see mounds of grass, the remains of Paddock Pond. Beyond the stream climb on the path into forest, shortly crossing a dilapidated fence on the left to reach open country. ② Continue upwards here, forest on the right, for a considerable time on a steady, and let's face it, increasingly boring slog with only slowly varying views of Djouce off to the left. At the crest of the hill you will meet a Wicklow Way waymark. Walk downhill until you reach a sizeable indentation in the forest (you should be able to see another waymark at its far end).

③ At this point you will have to decide whether to continue downhill and so complete the entire walk or whether to take the short variation, which simply consists of turning right to follow the forest edge on the right to a large, white quartzite stone, here following the commentary in the second last paragraph below. If you have the time (about 1 hour), don't mind the bracken prevalent in the height of summer and rough, wet ground then why not tackle the main route, as the lonely ambience of Glensoulan is worth experiencing.

For the main route, walk down to a bridge over a stream. This is the infant Dargle and it is here preparing itself for its precipitous plunge over cliffs as Powerscourt Waterfall. Do not cross the bridge; instead walk upstream along an intermittent path into the narrow steep-sided valley of Glensoulan with Djouce on the left and Maulin on the right.

You can wander as far as you like upstream - don't forget you have to walk

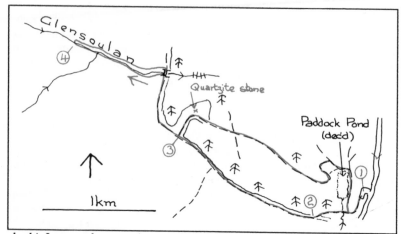

back! I suggest however that you ford a major tributary, beyond which are curious grassy hummocks and the occasional tree sheltering along the riverbank. ④ Ford the Dargle itself at about these hummocks and return along the northern bank. There's no particular reason to return on this bank rather than the other, by the way. However even a little variety might add a modicum of spice.

Cross the bridge close to forest and walk upwards to the major indentation noted earlier. ③ Turn left at the far (upper) end of the indentation, so that forest is close on the right. If you follow the track (or firebreak) here it will lead you into forest at a point where the quartzite stone on the left (noted above) acts as a useful reassurance.

From here on it's plod, plod, plod, most of the way on track in forest. Continue straight ahead at a crosstracks, wind downhill and at the first tee, turn right (just before this turn you will see your track down on the right and you can take a rough path down to it if you wish). This will take you across the end of the deceased Paddock Pond on the right. At the far side, turn right and walk the length of the pond, where you will recognise the path on which you started. Turn left for the nearby carpark.

ROUTE 14: UPPER LOUGH BRAY

The corrie lakes of Upper and Lower Lough Bray are two sparkling jewels set in a dull backcloth, the bogland stretching away to the west and south. Some lovely prospects but generally very muddy ground. A good area for leisurely pottering.

Getting There: Take the *Military Road* towards (not to) Sally Gap. Pass the acute right turn for Enniskerry (signposted) near the hamlet of Glencree and park in the

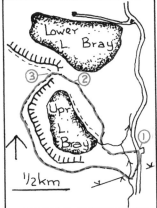

disused quarry on the left 1.7 miles further on.

Difficulties: Much wet ground, so boots are necessary even after a dry spell. Try not to widen the muddy patches, even if means walking right through them. Navigation is easy.

Walking Time: 1¼ hours (distance 3.5km, climb 150m).

Route: Most of the route, running along the skyline above the Upper Lough, is visible from the carpark. As you can see, it's not a route of hidden subtleties: its attractions are evident from here.

① Cross the road at the quarry and take the path beyond steeply down towards the Upper Lough. You will cross two streams and after the second you will have to make a choice of whether to keep right and walk along high ground above the lake or left and walk along the lakeshore. Whichever you choose makes little difference to the length of the route.

② The two paths converge at high ground overlooking both lakes: the Lower Lough is particularly scenic, with the house and woods on its far shore as its focal point. Contemplating the type of money required nowadays to buy such a house will take your mind off the next and hardest section of the walk, the climb to the Eagle's Crag.

The way up would be obvious even if there weren't a path. It's steep but not dangerous and ends just above great slabs of granite forming the wedge between the two lakes. Walk a few more metres above these slabs to gain gently sloping ground stretching away to Kippure, whose masts are visible above the bogland to the west. Incidentally, you might like to turn right and take the path above the *Lower* Lough on a there-and-back, though the route proper turns left to circle the Upper Lough.

③ There is a path of sorts along its top that tends to divide and re-form so that it is impossible to give exact directions. However the important points are to keep the Upper Lough on the left and not to lose too much height. With these in mind you will eventually head for the Military Road and see the electricity masts running to Kippure ahead. Still on a path head to the electricity mast nearest the road and follow it across a stream and onto tarmac. The quarry is only 100m or so down the road to the left.

ROUTE 15: PRINCE WILLIAM'S SEAT

A route mostly over subdued, heathery hillsides. The initial walk through, and then directly uphill alongside, forest ends high above Glencree, with the broad crest of the hills close on one side and with good views across Glencree to rocky Maulin. The walk ends on paths and tracks through mature forest.

Getting There: Drive to *Enniskerry*, turn right in the village towards Glencree. Park at the entrance to Curtlestown Forest on the right 3 miles from the village.

Bus: Take the Shop River variant of the 185. Check the time of the return bus.

Difficulties: None.

Walking Time: 2½ hours (distance 7km, climb 300m) for the main route; 1¾ hours (distance 5km, climb 240m) for the variation.

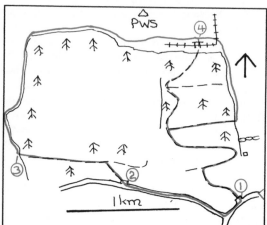

Route: ① Walk onward along the road away from Enniskerry and, ignoring a minor road on the left, walk to the next forest entrance about 1km away. That's the really dull part done.

② Take the forest track here, turn left at the nearby tee, and walk the track through mature trees, which nonetheless give several pleasant glimpses into Glencree. At the track's end continue resolutely onward for a few metres through the trees to open ground.

③ Navigation from here until further notice is simple: keep forest, young or mature, on the right. You will consequently first ascend nearly to the crest of the hill, the spur between Knocknagun and Prince William's Seat (you should see the tor marking Knocknagun behind). Then walk an undulating course on a fire-break close to this crest; a nice stretch with the crags and buttresses of Raven's Glen prominent across Glencree

④ When you encounter a few Wicklow Way waymarks do not follow the Way; instead round the forest to walk directly down the slope on a rough path, forest still on the right. When you get within about 100m of a stone wall turn into the forest through a clear break and so reach a nearby track (this avoids dreadful vegetation ahead on the direct descent). Take the track to the Wicklow Way, turn left and walk it to the start.

Short Variation: A route which has nearly as much climbing as the main route without the high-level walk. From the forest entrance where you started, walk the Wicklow Way until you emerge from forest and then follow the above commentary back to the start.

ROUTE 16: GLENCREE -- KNOCKREE

The tiny hill of Knockree rises incongruously from Glencree. The Wicklow Way crosses its southern and western shoulders and this easy walk follows it to give good though only slowly changing views across Glencree and the mountains to its south.

Getting There: Car to *Enniskerry*. Turn right in the village and follow the signs for the youth hostel. Pass the hostel to park at the Wicklow Way sign just beyond it. **Bus:** Take the Shop River variant of the 185. Check the time of the return bus.

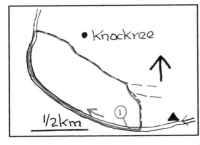

Difficulties: None.

Walking Time: ¾ hour (distance 3km, climb 150m).

Route: ① Childishly simple. Walk onward (west) along the narrow road flanked by walls of huge stones and the occasional clump of trees. Turn right off the road at a Wicklow Way waymark pointing onto a forest track and take it high above Glencree to give similar but more elevated views to those enjoyed on the outward leg. Continue on the Way where it swings right downhill to tarmac and the starting point.

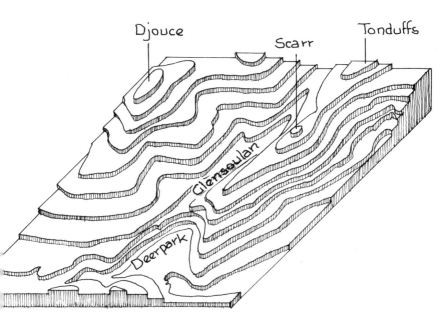

LOUGHS TAY AND DAN

A magnificent area of rugged mountains and cliffs around Loughs Tay and Dan, two of the loveliest lakes in the mountains. Most of the walks are pleasant underfoot (easy path or track), though they have varying degrees of climbing.
All parts may be easily reached by car from Dublin, but the bus service is poor. There is a 'bird's eye' view of part of this area on page 37.

ROUTE 17: CLOGHOGE AND INCHAVORE RIVERS

A low-level A to B walk into Cloghoge valley and around the western end of Lough Dan, where with little excessive effort you can enjoy a lovely blend of mountain, lake and wood from close to, though without the wider panorama that a higher-level walk would provide.

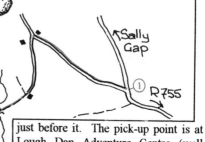

Getting There: Drive to *Kilmacanoge*, turn right here towards Glendalough and about 7 miles further on turn right onto the R759. After about two miles drop the walkers at the tarmac road on the left flanked by prominent gate pillars ('Pier Gates') and *not* at the track just before it. The pick-up point is at Lough Dan Adventure Centre (well signposted). It is reached by driving back downhill, taking the first turn right and then following signs for Lough Dan. The total distance from Dublin to Pier Gates is about 26 miles. A **bus** variation is given below. If you are travelling by bus don't forget that you can combine this route with route 22.

Difficulties: Some wet ground and an indistinct path in places. One river to cross which may be difficult after rain. Navigation quite straightforward.

Walking Time: 2½ hours (distance 8km, climb 120m).

Route: Easily described. ① Take the tarmac road down to the valley floor, cross two adjacent bridges and following signs for Lough Dan walk to the two-storey house on the Inchavore River.

② From here continue on a path along the northern shore of Lough Dan, with the steep slopes and later cliffs of Knocknacloghoge on the right. Keep straight ahead at the end of the lake, following the Inchavore River upstream through a marshy area where the path temporarily loses its way. At about 1¼ hours from the start you will reach the old deciduous trees of the copse, partly surrounded by ubiquitous conifers.

③ The one difficult feat in this walk is to ford the stream at the copse. That done, walk downstream following the river closely at first and then keeping fields

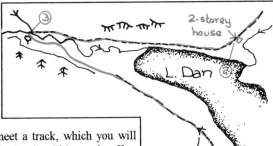

on the left so as to meet a track, which you will see climbing the hill ahead. This track offers lovely views down onto Lough Dan and the opposite shore. Keep an eye out for a gate on the left with a path beyond it, and take this rather than following the track. At its end turn left onto tarmac and walk to the small parking place at the Adventure Centre, a matter of a few hundred metres on the road.

Variation From Lough Dan: A there-and-back to the copse makes a lovely walk. From *Roundwood* follow signs for Lough Dan and park carefully at the Adventure Centre, as the road beyond it is narrow and there is no suitable parking place. Walk onward along the road, cross a bridge where the road swings left and becomes a track. Walk the track for a few metres, turning right through a narrow gate opposite the house 'Carrigeen Lodge' and take the path beyond high above the shores of Lough Dan. The path ends at a track onto which you turn right, pass an occupied house from which you can see your destination, the copse. This small clump of deciduous trees is backed by young conifers and there are older conifers clothing the slopes on its left, but is still distinctive.

Descend to the track's end and then walk through fields to reach an intermittent path running along the bank of Inchavore River as far as the copse itself. The walking time to the copse is about 40 minutes, with about 50 minutes for the return.

Bus Variation: This walk can be done using the St Kevin's Bus, but check times. Get the bus to the junction of the R755 and R759, take the R759 (Sally Gap road) here and walk about 3km mostly uphill to Pier Gates (about ¾ hour). Take the above main route to the Adventure Centre and then continue into Roundwood for the evening bus (about 1½ hours on tarmac to end). The walks at each end, while hardly exciting, are quite scenic in a modest kind of way.

ROUTE 18: SALLY GAP ROAD TO LOUGH DAN

There are few lovelier sights than that from Sally Gap road looking towards the mountains dominated by the great cliffs of Fancy. The walk down to Lough Dan on a scenic track, gradually modifies and expands this panorama. The return is a higher version of the outward stretch with wider views. A memorable walk.

Getting There: Drive to *Kilmacanoge*, turn right here towards Glendalough and about 7 miles further on turn right onto the R759. Less than two miles uphill park at a forest entrance on the left. The distance from Dublin is about 26 miles.

Difficulties: Moderately rough ground in parts.

Walking Time: 2¼ hours (distance 7km, climb 220m).

Route: ① From the forest entrance turn left to walk uphill for 100m or so and then turn left again onto a gated track. The navigation from here all the way to Lough Dan about 3km away is simple: a track overlooking some of the best scenery in Wicklow including a wealth of peaks and two large lakes: Lough Tay (over to the right at the start) and Lough Dan (ahead for much of the way).

As you near Lough Dan private property bars the way ahead. Turn right here onto a path and so reach the Inchavore River opposite a two-storey house. A good place for a rest. ② That done, walk the path back to the track, turn left onto it (there's no alternative) and right onto a grassy track just before the first ramshackle ... er ... shack on that side. At the first hairpin bend on this steep track ignore a track to the right and continue moderately upward to cross a gate at a point where there are stone walls running every which way on the left.

③ Beyond this gate the track is much less clear but runs gently uphill across the slope, so heading for a forestry plantation ahead, *not* the one off to the right at the crest of the hill. When you reach this plantation turn right onto a good track to cross a prominent gate, beyond which is forest.

④ Turn left immediately off the track to walk a narrow path, close to a fence separating high trees on the left from lower trees on the right. After a few minutes, and now there are no trees on the left, you will be able to cross this fence and take to a rough path. Simply keep to this path, forest on the right and heathery ground on the left, which allows unimpeded views across to Knocknacloghoge and Fancy. This will take you back to the road, where a right turn takes you to the forest entrance.

ROUTE 19: THE CLOGHOGE RIVER VALLEY

Overlooked by the fine peaks of Fancy (595m) and Knocknacloghoge (534m) and drained by the Cloghoge River and its tributaries, this valley probably embraces the loveliest scenery in all Wicklow. The Guinness family, who own the entire area, generously allow visitors. Leave the area, as indeed all others covered by this book, in at least a good a condition as you found it.

Since this is an area for leisurely pottering and because of the rugged nature of the mountains around you are mostly confined to there-and-back walks on the valley floor (but see also routes 17 and 18). Three such walks, which may be combined, are described below.

Getting There: Drive to *Kilmacanoge*, turn right here towards Glendalough and about 7 miles further on turn right onto the R759. After about two miles park around the two prominent gate pillars on the left ('Pier Gates'). This is a popular parking point and the road is narrow so park carefully. The total distance from Dublin is about 26 miles.

Routes: What all routes in this area have in common is a descent of nearly 200m at the start and unless you expire, the same climb at the end. The walk back from the bridge mentioned below should take at least 30 minutes *and this time is not included* in the times given below. Remember that before you venture too far!

Take the narrow tarmac road between the gate pillars and follow it all the way down to the valley floor. Having crossed one wide bridge you have three options.

Option 1: You can continue straight ahead to cross another bridge and make your way on track down to Lough Dan, passing by steeply sloping ground below Knocknacloghoge on one side and Cloghoge River on the other. When you reach the two-storey house near the lake (about 20 minutes to the bridges each way) you can take a continuation path along the lake shore into the valley of Inchavore River.

Option 2: You can turn right to cross a substantial stile, initially keep a stone wall close on the left and then take a continuation track running west into the wooded valley of Cloghoge Brook. The track is about 1km long and gradually rises, with the steep, rocky ground of Fancy on the right and the equally steep, rocky ground of Knocknacloghoge on the left. At its end you can follow Cloghoge Brook into remote country towards the Military Road. Though there is no path and the ground is rough, once you follow the stream you cannot get lost.

Option 3: You can cross the substantial stile and turn right immediately to pass by a fenced-off area. Beyond it keep Cloghoge River on the right and head on an intermittent path to reach the shores of Lough Tay, where you can wander along the shore until you are blocked by huge boulders at the foot of the great cliffs falling from the summit of Fancy right to the shores of Lough Tay. An inspiring spot, which it should take less than a half-hour to walk each way. On no account disturb residents in the nearby Luggala House.

ROUTE 20: SCARR AND BARTON'S WOOD

The initial climb with rough ground underfoot is brightened by unexpected vistas of lake and mountain glimpsed between trees and rocky outcrops. Beyond the scattered copse of Barton's Wood, high on the shoulder of Scarr (641m), the views are not quite so lovely and only slowly varying but the easy walking should compensate. Please, no dogs.

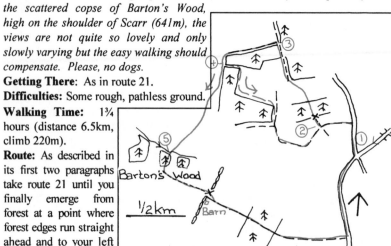

Getting There: As in route 21.

Difficulties: Some rough, pathless ground.

Walking Time: 1¾ hours (distance 6.5km, climb 220m).

Route: As described in its first two paragraphs take route 21 until you finally emerge from forest at a point where forest edges run straight ahead and to your left uphill.

③ Turn left to climb the short distance to the top corner of the forest, turn left again here and at the wide firebreak (④) just beyond this corner you will have to decide whether to do the main route or the easy variation (see below).

For the main route walk a little further alongside the forest until you can see slightly to your right the scattered trees of Barton's Wood peeping over the hillside. It is only a short distance to it but there is only an intermittent path. What with gorse and bracken to cross as well as a stream close to the border of the Wood, this is not the easiest of terrain. As you advance look out beyond the Wood for a path running on the level to an enormous barn, as this will be your next target.

Barton's Wood is a good place for a picnic (clear up after you!). From here, if the weather is good and you know what you are about you might like to climb to the top of Scarr, which should take about 1¼ hours there and back. Well, not exactly back because you should keep the Wood well to the left on the descent.

⑤ The route from the Wood is easy both underfoot and navigationally. Walk the path already mentioned to the barn, where you will meet the end of a rough track. Take it down through a band of low forest and beyond this to the road. Turn left here to walk along an attractive country road (attractive enough to be the route of the Wicklow Way) and turn first left for the start.

Easy Variation: Not the most inspiring of routes. Walk along the firebreak, turn right at its nearby end to follow the forest edge round two corners. At the far end of the second edge you will meet a track onto which you turn right. Take it all the way down to tarmac and turn right for the nearby start.

ROUTE 21: LOUGH DAN - THE WESTERN SLOPES

A gentle ascent through varied country ends in a remote, shallow valley between Scarr (641m) and its rocky northern spur. From most parts of the route there are excellent views down into Lough Dan and across to the mountains around it. Little climbing overall but some rough ground underfoot.

Getting There: Drive to *Roundwood*. Turn right here following the signs for Lough Dan. Turn right again just after a bridge about 2½ miles from Roundwood, still following signs for Lough Dan, and park immediately on waste ground on the left. The total distance from Dublin is 29 miles.

Difficulties: Some very muddy ground and a section of path bordered by (or indeed encroached on by) gorse. Navigation generally easy though care required in parts.

Walking Time: 1½ hours (distance 5km, climb 120m), though it can easily be extended.

Route: ① Walk towards Lough Dan, taking the nearby first turn left onto a gravel road. After walking 5 minutes or so and having just passed the first house on the right (the first at the time of writing, anyway) look out for a grassy track on the left ending at a nearby ruin and a similar track on the right ending at a gate that is not immediately visible from the track you are on.

② Pass through this gate and shortly emerge from the trees to be faced by more trees across a field. Cross this field and keep the trees on the right to follow a rough path. This path in turn enters another band of forest and at its nearby end at a corner of forest you will have the satisfaction of knowing that forest is behind and that the views, good so far when not obscured by trees, can now be enjoyed to the full.

③ From the forest keep straight ahead on a track and at its nearby end continue on a rough path through gorse, so heading for a farmhouse. Take the narrow lane on the left of the house (leave gates as you found them and walk quietly) and continue on the renewed path into the valley of Carrigeenshinnagh, keeping all the while close to increasingly rough fields on the right.

This is a lovely area: the rocky, hummocky ridge of Kanturk on the right, the high shoulder of Scarr on the left and ahead high, rough ground which leads to the nearby Military Road. You can wander as far as you like up the valley into increasingly remote country, but just to give form to the walk, I suggest the following. As you walk up the valley watch out for a dense clump of trees across the stream on the right, a little upstream of the last farmhouse in the valley. ④ Walk round the last of the upland fields to cross the infant stream just upstream of this clump. Turn right onto the path above it and then skirt the last farmhouse by keeping it well on the right.

⑤ When you reach the track beyond this farmhouse you can at last forget about navigation. Simply continue downhill to reach the end of the road and walk it about 1km to the start. By the way, it is well worthwhile to walk the path beyond the narrow gate opposite the house 'Carrigeen Lodge' for a few hundred metres to gain even better views of Lough Dan (this is route 17, variation).

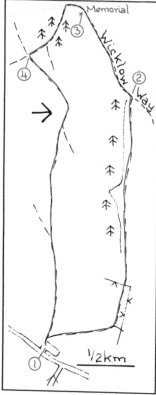

ROUTE 22: BALLINASTOE

A none too short slog up to White Hill, heather-clad terrain changing only slowly, ends in a vista of rugged mountain magnificence culminating in the deep bowl containing Lough Tay. The return is through a mostly clear-felled area with pleasant views over Calary Plateau.

Getting There: By car drive to *Kilmacanoge*, here taking the R755 towards Glendalough. Turn right after 5.7 miles and left at the nearby tee. Park in the forest entrance on the right a short distance away. This point may also be easily reached from *Enniskerry* by following the signs for Roundwood. In theory the start is accessible from the St Kevin's bus, but unless you intend to combine this route with route 17, which would make an all-day walk, the long journey by bus to and from the start hardly seems justifiable.

Difficulties: Some boggy patches might demand boots. Navigation is easy.

Walking Time: 2 hours (distance 6km, climb 260m).

Route: ① Turn right out of the carpark and right again onto another track a few metres up, Follow it to an electricity line. Turn left here and start slogging upward, forest and clear-felled area at first on both sides and later forest on the left only. As you ascend along the straight track the views behind open out, albeit a trifle reluctantly, to reveal Great Sugar Loaf and the wide expanse of Calary, while rolling heathery moorland gradually unfolds more and more of Djouce off to the right.

When you reach a distinct kink in the line of the forest you have done most of the climbing. A little farther on a Wicklow Way post heralds the Way and gives a good opportunity to rest and admire a wide panorama of mountains suddenly revealed. ② Then follow the Way south, that is turn left from the direction of the upward slog, anticipating that glorious moment when the sombre waters of

Lough Tay are revealed below the cliffs of Luggala. Take care, however to keep your feet firmly on the ground, and add as little as you can to the spreading quagmire underfoot.

③ When you pass the memorial to JB Malone, beautifully situated opposite Luggala cliffs and Lough Tay, it is time to pay attention to navigation. Keep on the Wicklow Way as it enters a short band of gloomy forest, ignore the minor track on the left when you emerge and at the nearby tee (or cross tracks if you count the grassy track running ahead) turn left where the Wicklow Way turns right (if you want to do route 17 follow the Wicklow Way).

④ You are now on a straightforward route back to the start. Shortly after leaving the Way you reach a clear-felled area and can see your route sweeping gracefully rightward across the hillside ahead. So, with this overall plan you will know to ignore the gravely track coming in on the right and to branch right later, thus continuing downhill. This track will lead you through a variety of conifers and cleared areas towards the edge of upland fields, and thence straight back to the carpark.

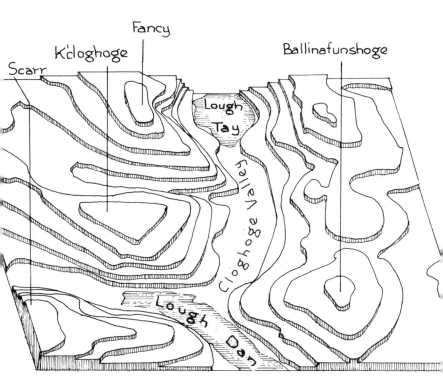

THE BLESSINGTON AREA

Though worthwhile peaks can be climbed in most of the routes, this is a rather quiet area in which good walks are a little difficult to find because of wide expanses of bogland and forest. The large Pollaphuca Reservoir (route 23) mitigates this lack of variety, while far to the south is the attractive bowl of the Glen of Imaal (route 25). The riverbank walks (routes 24, 27) give a good idea of the expanses of bogland in the area without risking navigational problems. Not a good area for public transport, with buses rarely venturing from the N81, and so too far from the mountains for the best walks.

ROUTE 23: LUGNAGUN AND SORREL

Varied terrain in an area not particularly noted for it, with long views across Pollaphuca Reservoir and the mountains of the north-west of the range, and with upland fields and gently sloping moorland closer at hand. Best walked in August when the heather is blooming. The variation to Sorrel Hill greatly expands the mountain panorama.

Getting There: Car to *Blessington*. Turn left after the Downshire Hotel, turn right shortly to cross the bridge over the reservoir and right again at the other side. From here follow the signs for Lacken for a further 1.8 miles, here taking a narrow road on the left, signposted as a cul-de-sac, to the forest entrance about a half-mile up.

Difficulties: Some rough ground and a difficult fence near the end which may be avoided (but you will have to decide this in advance). A few easy fences near the start, which may have been reinforced by the time you walk, though I have no evidence to support this.

Walking Time: 1¾ hours (distance 6km, climb 200m).

Route: ① Take the forest track to the nearby first bend (it's to the right) here taking to forest on the left to walk on a rough path between trees to open ground a little way off. Once there, turn right uphill, forest close on the right, to make the only steep climb of the walk. Along here you might like to combine the occasional rest with a study of the scene behind: Pollaphuca Reservoir, an undulating field system and the town of Blessington in the middle distance.

After crossing two fences the focus of attention switches to Sorrel Hill ahead, (it's crowned by a massive cairn) along with an ever-widening array of generally bland peaks. Continue with the forest edge always on the right, negotiating a few more easy fences, until you reach the corner of the forest and must make the decision whether to press on to Sorrel Hill (see below).

② If you have decided to walk the main route, turn right downhill, still following the forest edge, and after about 3 minutes cross into forest at a hairpin bend in a forest track, turning left onto it. Take a note of the time here because you will be leaving this track in about 10 minutes.

Or maybe you won't, because you can simply continue down this track to the start. However if you wish to get some good views of the Reservoir and do not mind the imposing fence you have to cross, look out on the left for a stile clearly visible from the forest track. ③ Cross the stile and turn right to take a rough path beyond it heading diagonally right downhill, or if you fail to locate it head across upland fields for the nearby corner of forest.

Cross the gate at this forest corner and follow the firebreak beyond, forest close on the right. In a few minutes you will reach the fence mentioned already, beyond which a track is visible. You may have to seek out a place along the forest edge to gain this track, and when you do so you may be consoled to know that your problems are over. For now all you have to do is follow the track, which later improves to a road and leads directly back to the start.

Hard Variation: The climb to Sorrel is worthwhile if the day is clear (and likely to remain so) because of the wide panorama visible from it. You can follow an earthbank most of the way to the huge summit cairn and then retrace your steps to the corner of forest. The extra walking time is about 1¼ hours (distance 3km, climb 180m).

Note

The construction of Pollaphuca Reservoir began in the early 1940's. Although no villages were inundated 76 families had to move and the two villages of Ballyknockan and Valleymount, both now close to the reservoir, found themselves much further away by road. During the very dry summer of 1978 some previously submerged homesteads re-emerged eerily from the depths. Curiously, at the wane of one of the ice ages an even larger lake, fed by melting snow, occupied the area now covered by this man-made feature. When the resulting water finally escaped southwards it left behind the great gash of the Hollywood Glen (route 26).

ROUTE 24: GLENREEMORE AND ART'S CROSS

Easy track through conifers and clear-felled areas to start and then a gentle walk upstream into remote, open country with rocky spurs on both sides. The return is a struggle over rough ground along the banks of two swiftly flowing, scenic rivers.

Getting There: By car from the west take the N81 past *Blessington*, turn left onto the R756 (Wicklow Gap Road), pass the old schoolhouse on the right after about 5 miles (you'll recognise the old Irish lettering over the door), continue for another 2.2 miles to turn right (the only junction on this side for miles) and park just past the nearby bridge. The total distance from Dublin is 32 miles.

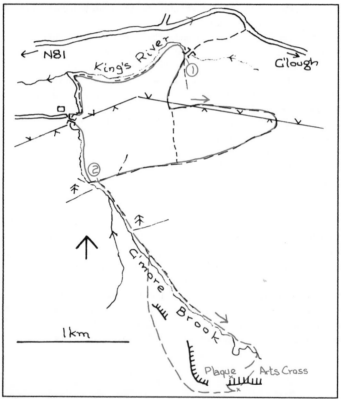

Difficulties: Easy on the initial forest tracks, muddy along the lower Glenreemore Brook and rough underfoot for much of the final kilometre. The variation is partly through pathless terrain that can be quite remote and frightening in bad visibility so a map and compass is essential.

Walking Time: 1½ hours (distance 5.5km, climb 80m) for the main route. The variation should take about 3½ hours (distance 10km, climb 420m).

Route: ① At the bridge ignore the left fork, which ends at a house, and take the forest track to the first bend under the giant pylons. Here you might like to try a short-cut if you abhor conifers. If so, leave the track at this bend to walk directly uphill on a steep, pathless route and at the first track turn right to rejoin the route. The last time I was there I was pleasantly surprised that I could make quite easy progress, even though there were some branches underfoot; on other trips this has been hard going. Maybe you will be lucky.

Paragons of orthodoxy will should continue on the track around a bend and then generally on the level to reach Glenreemore Brook at trees well set back from its bank. ② Here you can turn left and wander as far as you like into increasingly remote and rugged country following the river bank all the way. This way also leads to the hard variation (see below). Alternatively you can turn right for home, the main route, which in spite of the short distance should take about 40 minutes because of difficult underfoot conditions.

Let's describe the main route first. Walk downstream to pass under the pylons, cross a rough bridge, turn right and cross the same stream on stepping stones. (This seems daft, but the alternative means crossing a fence.) Continue to walk downstream to an area of stunted-looking conifers, veering right where thick vegetation hides the junction of Glenreemore Brook, which you have been following and King's River, which you want to follow.

③ You will know that you have passed this junction because you are now walking upstream and the river is considerably wider. The underfoot conditions are still poor on an intermittent path, so make sure you do not tumble into the waters. At length you will reach a less intermittent path, enter a block of forest and, keeping the river within reach on the left, cross a wall and reach amenity planting. The bridge which you drove across lies directly ahead.

Hard Variation: If you walk uphill along the river bank for about 45 minutes you will come to a boggy, enclosed plateau, about which the sluggish Glenreemore Brook wanders in tight loops. Cross the river here to find nearby Art's Plaque, a simple inscription on slabs. From here you can climb steeply on a grassy ramp to Art's Cross, which is directly above the Plaque (you will have seen the Cross on your walk up the valley). ④ From the Cross you can keep to the high ground by walking west for a few hundred metres and then swinging north. You can continue down the spur for as long as you like, but don't forget you have to cross the Glenreemore Brook, so don't leave it too far down its course. At forest you rejoin the main route near point ②.

ROUTE 25: LOBAWN

Lobawn (636m) is the mountain which embraces the Glen of Imaal on the north.
This long walk (the variation is much shorter) up the eastern spur of Lobawn
and round on a high level route to nearby Sugarloaf gives excellent views of the
varied country around the Glen and across to the Lugnaquillia massif.

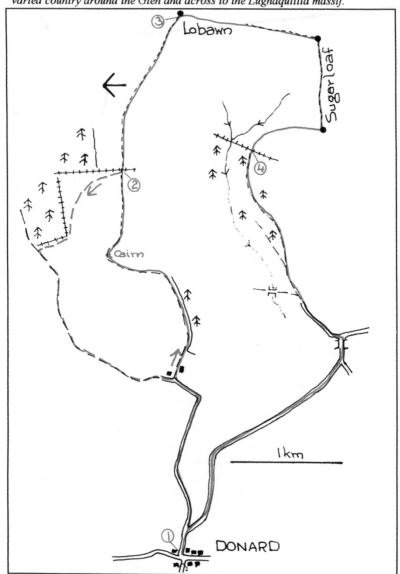

Getting There: Drive to *Donard* and park in the village.

Difficulties: The main route includes some walking on rough pathless ground so you will need a map and compass. There is some high heather on the variation.

Walking Time: 4¼ hours (distance 13km, climb 480m) for the main route (extra time is needed for one steep descent but this is more than offset by lots of road walking), and 3 hours (distance 9km, climb 400m) for the variation, where extra time for rough terrain is offset by road walking.

Route: ① From the village take the road signposted for the youth hostel for a few hundred metres, and fork first left, indicating Kilcoagh. This is a narrow country road lined by lovely old trees and makes for a delightful walk. At the road's end is a farmyard. Turn right up a track just inside the yard and, ignoring the entrance to a house, keep on the track to cross the second of two adjacent gates on the left.

Continue up the track into open country with a dense forestry plantation on the right and upland fields on the left, beyond which is the valley of the alliterative if tautologous Browns Beck Brook. The track curves gently up around the shoulder of Lobawn as far as a cairn fairly high on its western spur, where it is replaced by a path roughly following a fence on the right. Continue climbing gently on this path until you reach a fence across your path. If you wish to do the variation do not cross it (see below).

② However if the day is good and you know what you are about continue gently upward and eastward following the fence and later a rough ditch to Lobawn. On this climb you will see a good section of the Wicklow mountains, with Lugnaquillia crowning all off to the south-east, easily recognisable because of the great corrie of the North Prison gouged out of its near side.

The summit of Lobawn (636m) is crowned by a pillar bearing the cryptic message WD 13. Now look south from here. You will see the two gently rising summits of Sugarloaf near at hand, with the bulk of Keadeen between and towering above them. ③ The plan now is to walk to the two Sugarloafs, initially on a pathless stretch. However the terrain of fairly soft bog should present no difficulties and the gradient is ideal, practically all on the level.

About half-way to the first Sugarloaf you will pick up a path which will take you to the first summit, which has a fallen WD pillar on its modest summit. The path turns sharply right here to reach the cairn on the second.

So far, so good. The next section has no path but as long as you are walking roughly north you will meet either a forest on the left or a stream on the right, more likely the latter. Let's assume therefore that you reach a point where you can see the stream below. Turn left to follow it to the forest, where a little diligent searching may be needed to find a weak section of fencing and a faint but clear path heading directly into the scattered trees beyond it. From this point also you should be able to see the confluence of three streams, the two bigger in tiny but deep valleys.

④ Take this path to reach a grassy track after a few minutes; with navigational worries behind you, you can now relax. Keep straight ahead to reach major track with a farm off on the right. Walk onward on this track to a narrow road, and at its end turn right onto tarmac and walk about 2km back into Donard.

Easier Variation: From point ② above, turn left steeply downhill initially following the fence towards forest near at hand. As you descend through high heather veer away from this block of forest so that you are eventually walking parallel to another block down on the valley floor. Round this block to reach a clear track. Turn left onto it and take it past at least one muddy section to pass (quietly please) through the farmyard encountered on the outward leg. Return by the same narrow road to Donard.

ROUTE 26: HOLLYWOOD GLEN AND CHURCH MOUNTAIN

Pleasant but unspectacular views and only slowly unfolding scenery with, in places, long views over the plains of Kildare. Some forested areas, though mercifully much of it is mature and well-spaced or clear-felled, so that views are not too restricted. You can cut the route short by not climbing to the summit of Church (544m), though the views from it make it worthwhile.

Getting There: Car only. Take the N81 past *Blessington* for about 7 miles and then watch out for the R756 on the left. Don't take it. Instead continue straight ahead, and after 0.4 miles turn left onto a minor road, the first after the R756. Drive 1.1 miles to park at a forest entrance on the left. The total distance from Dublin is 27 miles.

Difficulties: Some wet patches and mud underfoot, otherwise easy.

Walking Time: 2¼ hours (distance 6km, climb 360m).

Route: ① Walk the forest track and at the nearby first junction, take the middle track, that is the one heading gently upward through a clear-felled area offering, initially at least, good views down into a narrow river valley. Ignore a minor track on the left to enter a narrow band of mature trees.

② Cross the gate at its end, turn right to a nearby ruin and here commence the climb directly upward to Church, on a track (or firebreak) with mature trees on the right, and not so mature trees on the left. ③ At the first junction, where there is also a turning circle on the left, you will have to make a decision whether to climb to the summit of Church, a simple there and back which should take about 1¼ hours.

If you do so decide, continue upward, emerge from forest (which enhances the views) and cross a fence near the summit. Now on a path, continue onward as it swings left. When it starts downhill leave it to reach the huge heaps of stones and trig pillar off to the right marking the summit. If there is any sign of bad visibility note carefully how you are going to get back to this path. The views from here are particularly good, embracing a wide range of the highest peaks in the mountains to north, east and south and the plains of Kildare to the west. Hope it was worth the toil of the ascent! Retrace your steps to the fence and then walk directly back to the turning circle passed on the ascent.

③ At the turning circle turn into dense forest, pass an acute junction on the left, follow the track out of forest round a great loop to the right and at the next junction, take the left option, or perhaps better described as continuing straight ahead. If you have any doubts that you are on the right track, a ruin on the left shortly after this junction should reassure you.

Shortly after this ruin the track swings right to reveal the great gash of Hollywood Glen down on the left, though to see more than just the top of it, it is necessary to divert a little from the track over rough ground. That done, continue downward on the track, ignoring side turns to reach the start.

ROUTE 27: BALLYDONNELL BROOK

A remote and quiet area of marginal farmland and gently sloping heather-covered moorland focused on Ballydonnell Brook and its several tributaries. Some forestry, much of it young and therefore unlikely to impede the views for some years to come. These views include varied angles on the valley of Ballydonnell Brook and further off brooding Mullaghcleevaun and other subdued peaks to the south.

Difficulties: The river bank that forms much of this route does not allow for a fast or even steady pace, but who cares? - this is an area for a leisurely stroll. Persons with any sensitivity will be appalled by the litter and other signs of an environmental 'couldn't care less' attitude evident near the start of this route.

Getting There: Drive towards *Blessington*, turning left onto the R759 just after Brittas. Follow the signs for Sally Gap for about 4 miles, then turn right to cross the nearby River Liffey. Turn first left, pass a cul-de-sac road on the left, and continue for another mile to park in the second of two closely spaced forest entrances on the left. The road for the last mile or so is exceedingly narrow, so take care. This point can also be reached from Blessington.

Walking Time: 1½ hours (distance 6km, climb 50m) but the walk can be extended further southward along a stream.

Route: ① From the forest entrance take the narrow road, not the forest track on its right. The road passes through a stretch of forest and, by now definitely no more than a track, shortly reaches a junction, with a forest track ahead and a track ending at a deserted farmhouse downhill on the left. Walk towards the farmhouse and if you are so inured to rubbish scattered everywhere that it no longer bothers you, pass through the yard and continue on down to the main river in the valley, Ballydonnell Brook. If you are with visitors and wish to impress them of the beauty of our countryside make some excuse and avoid this farmhouse by keeping it well on the left. When you reach the river, turn right and simply follow it upstream. A nice, quiet stretch, with the stream fronting undulating moorland on the left and upland fields and later young forestry on the right. You will pass in turn the confluence of two major tributaries with Ballydonnell Brook as you walk upstream, both coming in on the opposite bank: Lugaculleen Brook and Glenavadda Brook, both slicing through the moorland and so visible for some distance and both sheltering a few rowan trees along their banks. Between their confluence with Ballydonnell Brook you can use a bridge to cross the comparatively minor Dealbog Brook.

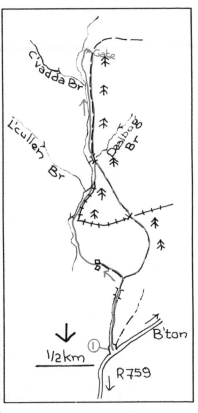

The beauty of walking upstream, anywhere, anytime, is that *you can't get lost*. This means that you can walk along any tributary in this shallow valley as far as you like. However, when you come to what appears to be an unnecessarily sturdy iron gate I suggest you turn back, as the scenery doesn't vary much from here on.

Turn right onto a forest track here. It rises a little above the valley floor and gives enhanced views of the valley and beyond, but don't expect anything spectacular. There is only one decision point; a junction where, having met it before, you will know to turn left.

GLENDALOUGH

Popular Glendalough is justly noted for its monastic settlements and lovely scenery. The rugged mountains overlooking the valley's two lakes give comparatively hard walks (routes 29-32) and their slopes easier strolls (routes 28, 33). Route 34's goal is a remote mountain lake. Glendalough is served only by St Kevin's bus, though easy to reach by car. . There is a 'bird's eye' view of part of this area on page 51.

ROUTE 28: THE UPPER LAKE

A there-and-back walk along the shore of the Upper Lake and into the valley beyond it, between the great boulders of Camaderry and the steeply rising grassy slopes of the Spink. On the return the views back to the Upper Lake are superb. An easy and deservedly popular walk, and a great area for leisurely picnics (but clear up after you!).

Getting There: Drive to *Glendalough*, pass the Royal Hotel on the left and continue on for less than 1 mile to park in the Upper Carpark (a small charge may be payable). By St Kevin's **bus** to the terminus, from where you can cross the footbridge in the cemetery containing the Round Tower and take the track along the south side of the valley to the start proper.

Difficulties: Some wet ground underfoot but nothing serious.

Walking Time: 2 hours (distance 7km, climb 200m) but the walk can be extended indefinitely westward along the river.

Route: It could hardly be easier. ① From the carpark take one of several routes to the nearby Upper Lake and from there walk the broad track along its shore, the lake on the left. Beyond the lake pass through old mine workings, where there may be some difficulty in finding a route around, over and between streams. After that climb the zig-zag track towards the gently-sloping valley of Glenealo, before which the track degenerates to a path.

This path runs along the main river of the valley and a little searching here will reveal a few delightful rocky pools backed by cascades and low waterfalls - lovely spots to linger. You can turn back anywhere and with the main river close on the left you can hardly go wrong, but I suggest that you don't go further than the huge heap of mining spoil on the far bank. Beyond that the valley opens out and the path is soggier. Unfortunately you must return by the same route but you can vary it marginally by taking the narrow path along the lakeshore rather than walking along the track.

ROUTE 29: CAMADERRY

Approaching Laragh on the R755 you will see ahead a great block of grassy mountain, bare but for a few scattered trees. This is Camaderry, separating the lovely valley of Glendalough from the much smaller valley of Glendasan to its north. The route takes in a little of Glendasan before contouring across the side of Camaderry, so giving lovely views down into Glendalough. An easy walk though the variation is much harder with much climbing.

Getting There: By car to *Glendalough.* Park in the Visitor Centre in the village (preferably - but note the closing time before you do so) or in the small carpark on the right just beyond the road bridge in the village and close to the cemetery containing the Round Tower. By St Kevin's **bus** to the terminus.

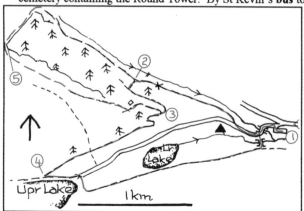

Difficulties: Some usually wet ground on the main route. Apart from the tough climb there is much rough ground underfoot on the hard variation.

Walking Time: The main route should take about 1¼ hours (distance 4km, climb 80m). The variation takes about 2½ hours (distance 7km, climb 240m), thus allowing some time for rough terrain.

Route: ① If you have parked in the Visitor Centre, turn left out of it, cross the road bridge, walk another 100m or so and here take the first track on the right to enter Glendasan and a much quieter world than Glendalough: rising fields on the left and the gently flowing Glendasan River on the right. After you pass a forest bar, watch out for rough stepping stones across the river. Walk only another 100m or so along the track and here (②) plunge into forest, following a path running directly upward if you come across it.

As you climb watch out carefully only a little way up for a secluded, narrow, grassy path heading gently diagonally upwards through the trees. Turn left onto it to regain open ground with fields down on the left, the same fields you passed earlier. ③ The path ends at a forest track onto which you turn left and follow all the way back gently downhill to the Upper Lake. All this stretch gives lovely views down through scattered mature conifers into the Lower and Upper Lakes in turn, with the wooded shoulder of Derrybawn across the narrow valley.

④ At length you will reach the main track running along the shore of the Upper Lake. Turn left onto it and at the end of the lake turn right to follow one of any number of paths and tracks to reach the track tucked in close to the densely wooded slopes of Derrybawn on the southern side of the narrow valley (it's a deservedly popular route and you are unlikely to mistake it). Turn left onto it to walk through ancient oaks and then close to the shores of the Lower Lake. Take the first footbridge on the left to reach the carpark close to the Round Tower or the nearby second footbridge to reach the Visitor Centre carpark.

Hard Variation: A much tougher proposition and one not to be attempted in late summer or autumn when the ferns are high.

Instead of turning off the track by the Glendasan River, continue along it to the end of the valley where the boundary of the forest on the left heads straight up-hill (views here are not enhanced by the old mining spoil close on the right). Follow the forest all the way to its upper corner where a stop to view a consider-able array of mountains might be in order even if your heart isn't demanding it.

⑤ The idea now is to turn left and follow the forest boundary, but not slavishly. If you are a little higher than the forest your views will be enhanced and it may aid in avoiding some of the high heather hereabouts which makes the going pretty wearing. It may be useful to know that there is a clear grassy path on the crest of the hill high up on the right, and you may like to struggle up to it. As you can see from the sketch map *it may not be the path you want*. If it swings decisively right down the slope it isn't, and you will have to continue along the crest of the high ground until you shortly reach another grassy path. This is the path you will certainly meet sooner or later if you keep close to the forest bound-ary. This latter path keeps to the crest of the hill and meets the end of a forest track, the track walked on the main route. Turn left onto it to shortly reach ③ in the above description.

ROUTE 30: THE SPINK

The view from the bold promontory of the Spink can scarcely be equalled in Wicklow: impressive mountains looming to north and west, the great cleft of upper Glendalough cradling the Upper Lake and the mighty rocky cliffs of Camaderry directly to the north. It's a slog to get to the Spink and there is a comparatively tame finish but overall this is one of the most scenic walks in Wicklow. A suitable area for dogs.

Getting There: By car to *Glendalough*. Park in the Upper Carpark beyond the village, where a small parking fee may be levied. By St Kevin's **bus** to the ter-minus.

Difficulties: Wet and boggy ground on part of the Spink, so boots are essential. Navigation is easy on the main route but the variation demands a clear day and careful attention to route directions.

Walking Time: 1¾ hours (distance 5km, climb 260m) for the main route. The variation takes 3½ hours (distance 9km, climb 420m), and is a lot more demanding.

Route: From the carpark you will readily observe the wooded shoulder of the Spink rising majestically from the southern shores of the Upper Lake. Even from here it is clear that the climb is going to be worthwhile.

① Walk across the sward from the carpark to cross the bridge over the Polla-nass River and then climb steeply on a path with the turbulent Pollanass Water-fall plunging valley-ward on the left. The path ends on a forest track. Here continue upward to a junction of tracks, where you should turn right and continue the upward advance. ② At the nearby first bend, a left, leave the track by taking a stile on the right and follow the rough path beyond first gently upward to mature forest and then steeply upward following this forest's edge. Cross two stiles to emerge on the crest of the Spink. Wasn't it worth the effort!

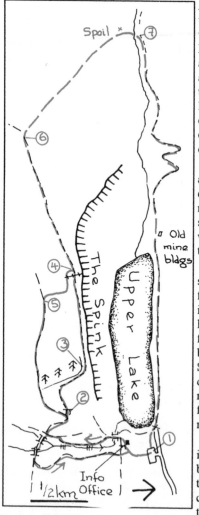

A short preview before you walk further. From here for about 1km you will walk poised above the Upper Lake, with the cliffs of Camaderry across the valley and an increasing array of mountains gradually revealing themselves. On a severely practical level: the path along here is very eroded and muddy, so as well as taking care of yourself make sure that you don't make it any worse.

③ Turn left (of course) and walk west along the Spink, keeping well clear of cliffs on the right. After the above mentioned kilometre you will meet a stile in a fence across your path and will have to decide whether to walk the main route or the tougher variation. ④ Assuming the main route, cross the stile and immediately turn left away from the lake to cross a fence. The idea now is to reach a forest track a little way down the slope directly away from the lake. There is no clear path, but if you walk initially back along the Spink for a few metres and then plunge directly downhill into forest where it is not so dense, you should reach the forest track without too many anxious moments.

⑤ Turn left onto the track and follow it down through scattered trees, right back to the junction of tracks met at the start of the walk. You can of course return by the outward route, but there is more variety in taking a slightly different one. At the junction, take the branch that bridges two closely-spaced streams and immediately fork left. This track will take you to the valley floor, with Pollanass Waterfall off on the left. Once there the carpark is a short distance away across the grass.

Tough Variation: Do not attempt this route after heavy rain (there is a stream to cross) and then only on a clear day (there is pathless terrain). Your reward will be lots of lovely views especially into Glenealo.

From the stile mentioned above continue along the Spink, now climbing fairly steeply. Surprisingly the path widens to a track (or firebreak) which borders scattered trees on the left. ⑥ Where the track swings left uphill, and you now have nearly 2 hours' walking under your belt, turn right off it onto heather, heading for the ramparts of Turlough Hill across the valley. (The exact point where you leave the track is not crucial, as long as you don't attempt it too early and so reach the cliffs on the south side of Glendalough.)

Heading for Turlough Hill will take you over level ground at first and then steeply down into Glenealo. As you descend, Turlough Hill disappears behind the shoulder of Camaderry; now head for a huge pile of mining spoil down in the valley. It should be easy to cross Glenealo River about here. ⑦ After which, turn right and head down the valley on a developing path and later track. Navigation is now simple, and the views of the cliffs of the Spink and Camaderry and later the waters of the Upper Lake to right, left and ahead respectively are marvellous. A memorable end to what should have been a satisfying walk.

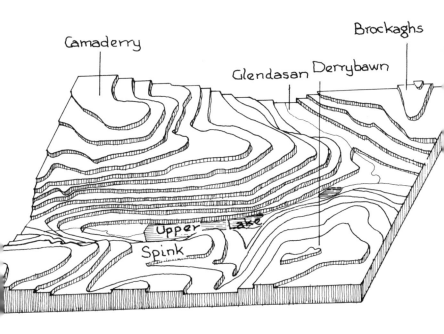

ROUTE 31: THE BROCKAGHS

The Brockaghs (470-557m) is the name for a group of rounded hills to the north-west of Laragh. The main route takes you into these hills and gives lovely, wide views and easy ground underfoot; naturally this involves a lot of climbing. The easy variation has much more forestry and therefore restricted views.

Getting There: Car or bus to *Laragh*. Cross the main bridge in the village, fork right immediately and turn right just before McCoys shop. Park at the forestry entrance on the right a few hundred metres further on.

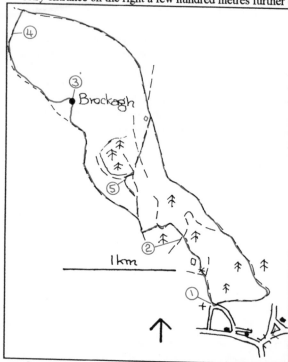

Difficulties: The climbing has already been mentioned. There is a little wet ground. In poor visibility it might be prudent not to attempt the main route as you might find yourself in frightening territory if you lose your path or track.

Walking Time: 2½ hours (distance 7.5km, climb 300m), excluding the small additional climb to reach the summit of Brockagh. The easy variation should take 1½ hours (distance 4.5km, climb 170m).

Route: The first part of the route is a bit tricky navigationally so take a little care.

① From the forestry entrance, keep the wall of the nearby church initially close on the left to walk up a track. Continue steadily upward, ignoring side turns and driveways to the sign indicating the driveway to 'Brockagh View'. Here take the path edged by moss-covered stone walls and reached through a wooden gate. You are now entering the territory of many (well, several) gates.

Walk up this path, keeping a deserted house on the left and crossing the gates already alluded to. The path, originally soft and muddy, assumes a pleasant, grassy surface for about 100m before finishing at another gate (of course) with a junction of forest tracks ahead.

② Continue straight ahead from this junction for another 100m or so and here, where there is a break in the forest on the left, ascend a rough path leading into open country and specifically onto a track heading upwards.

At this point you have progressed only a few hundred metres from the start but from here on navigation is much simpler and fewer words per metre travelled (so to speak) are necessary. The general idea now, if you are on the main route anyway, is to climb, keeping to a path or track (but the right one!) all the way.

So, with upland fields and then a small block of forestry on the right head steadily upward, keeping to any branch of track or clear path displaying a resolutely upward inclination. As you ascend the path (it is now certainly no more than that) keeps to the right of the highest ground and then swings left through a tiny pass with the summit of one of the Brockaghs on the right. If the day is good it is worthwhile leaving the path to reach the summit, which is adorned with an assemblage of huge boulders. The views are splendid with Glendalough particularly attractive. *However*, if you have any doubts at all that you are going to regain the path don't attempt this detour.

③ From the summit walk west to reach the path again and follow it across the crest of the ridge on level ground and then downward towards scattered trees. As you descend the path becomes more indistinct and steeper, so that by the time you reach a forestry fence it is heading directly down the slope and has all but disappeared.

④ Walk downward through the scattered trees to turn right onto a nearby forestry track. From here on navigation is easy and so allows you to concentrate on the scenery: initially back to Glenmacnass Waterfall and across to Scarr and later down into the deep valley of Glenmacnass. Navigation? Just walk downhill, keeping to the main track and ignoring branches heading either back or upward. The one point where you may have some doubts is at the tee near home, where you turn left.

Easy Variation: This is a lower version of the main route. The views are circumscribed by trees and higher ground near at hand but there is much less climbing and the chances of wandering off course are minimal.

Follow the main route into open country but instead of following the track or path along the highest ground, keep the forestry within reach on the right. ⑤ After about 20 minutes on path or rough track you will observe a block of forest rising alarmingly up the mountainside ahead and a notice down on your right. Head for this notice, cross the gate beyond it and walk downhill at the first junction and after that straight ahead for a few minutes. Watch out on the left for a ruin mouldering into undergrowth and turn right at the tee immediately beyond it. Now follow the directions given at the end of the main route.

ROUTE 32: DERRYBAWN RIDGE

There are few places in Wicklow where you can experience ridge walking, so that you have the pleasure of long-distance views on both sides. *The best of these is the narrow Derrybawn Ridge (474m) above Glendalough, where the long views on both sides are superb for about 1.5km and quite good thereafter. The one snag is the increasingly dull, straight track before you reach the ridge.*

Getting There: St Kevin's bus to Laragh followed by a pleasant walk on tarmac for about 40 minutes to the start proper. The variation given below ends in Glendalough so that you can get the bus back.

By car drive to *Laragh* and here take the R755 south, forking right after less than a mile towards Glenmalure. The starting point is the second of two closely

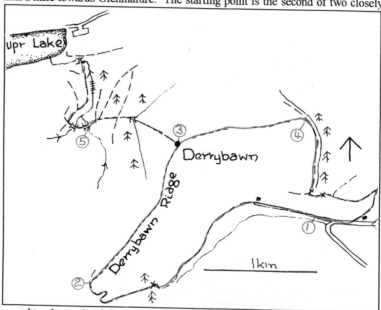

spaced tracks on the right about 0.6 miles from this fork. You can park on waste ground about 100m along this second track or you might prefer to keep to the main road, cross a bridge just after it and park a little way along on the right, where there is room for not more than two carefully parked cars.

Difficulties: Mostly good underfoot with only a few moderately damp patches. Though there is some pathless terrain, navigation is easy, except for one stretch (see below), for which a map and compass will be needed in bad visibility.

Walking Time: The main route is 2¼ hours (distance 7km, climb 320m); the variation, which ends in Glendalough and therefore involves the bus or a second car is also 2¼ hours (distance 6.5km, climb 300m).

Route: ① Assuming you have parked along the track, walk onward to pass the last house and continue gently uphill towards the head of the shallow valley. The rocky Derrybawn Ridge high on the right is the most attractive feature hereabouts; there is a lot of unvarying hillside in other directions. Trees have been recently planted on both sides of the track, surprisingly and gratifyingly many of them deciduous.

Having climbed a formidable gate you are into open and steeper country, though still in the same valley and still on the track. ② At nearly its end, a few despairing wriggles right at the foot of the Derrybawn Ridge, turn right off it to take a path running along the length of the ridge.

This long, bony finger reaches north-east with the Upper Lake of Glendalough way down on the left and a whole range of lofty peaks in all directions; navigation is easy as you need only keep to the well-defined high ground. You will note as you advance that the ridge swings distinctly right mid-way along its length, and the precise point at which you should turn is marked by a summit cairn - the summit in question being Derrybawn itself.

③ So, when you reach the cairn or just beyond it (at about 1½ hours) turn right, that is directly away from the Upper Lake and start along an intermittent path which keeps to the high ground. If in any doubt keep the distant cone of Great Sugar Loaf off to the left. The views along here, though good are not as fine as previously. This is partly because the ridge is wider and the hummocky terrain obscures some of the mountain scenery.

Your target on this stretch after the summit of Derrybawn Mountain is a forest track running alongside forest, and since it sweeps directly across your path you would have to be wildly out to miss it. ④ When you reach it turn right and take it gradually downhill to a tee. Turn left here to cross a nearby gate and enter forest. Just inside the forest you will meet a main forest track, where you continue straight ahead downhill. Continue on this main track to another tee where you turn right and right again on tarmac. Your car is up the first track on the right if you parked off the main road.

Alternative Route ending in Glendalough: This is undoubtedly a more satisfying route. Walk to the cairn on Derrybawn and then descend initially towards the Spink. From the cairn you will recognise this hill because its shoulder partially blocks the view of the Upper Lake. After a short distance you will pick up a narrow path heading directly downhill to forest. Cross the stile at the forest and take the path onward and steeply downhill across one track to turn left onto a second.

⑤ Cross two adjacent bridges and turn right downhill with the Pollanass Waterfall on the right. On the valley floor you have a choice (hope you made the rendezvous clear before you started) of being picked up at the Upper Carpark, where your unfortunate chauffeur may have to pay for parking, or at the Visitor Centre where he/she won't. If you are on the bus you have no choice: you will have to pick up the bus near the Visitor Centre. To get there turn right on the valley floor and walk the track to cross the main river in the valley by the first or second footbridges.

ROUTE 33: DERRYBAWN FOREST

Magnificent views down into Glendalough on a route exclusively on forest tracks and clear paths. A steep climb by Pollanass Waterfall leads to a long gentle incline and a leisurely walk back along the valley floor. This walk may easily be combined with route 30.

Getting There: Start from the Visitor Centre carpark, *Glendalough*, which may be easily reached by car or St Kevin's **bus**. If in the car, note the time the carpark closes.

Difficulties: None.

Walking Time: 2¼ hours (distance 8km, climb 150m).

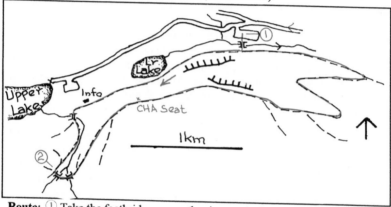

Route: ① Take the footbridge across the river at the back of the Visitor Centre's carpark to turn right onto the popular tree-lined track running along the south side of the valley. This track takes you past the Lower Lake and the Information Office. After it, cross a bridge on the left and continue on a footpath close beside the turbulent Pollanass Waterfall.

After a stiff but short climb you will join a forest track. Continue upwards for a short distance to reach a cross tracks. ② Turn left here, so crossing two bridges close together between which is a pillar displaying samples of local rock. Ignoring a minor fork on the left just beyond the bridges keep straight ahead where a branch heads acutely right. Beyond this branch there is a sturdy seat erected by the CHA, where you can enjoy lovely views down into Glendalough without even having to stand.

Thus refreshed, continue onward and gently upward through mature and well-spaced trees which hardly impair the views. As for navigation, all you have to remember is to fork left at the next two junctions and so reach the valley floor at a track running along the edge of an ancient oakwood. Turn left onto this track and right over the first bridge, the one you crossed at the start of the walk.

ROUTE 34: LOUGH OULER

If you enjoy walks along streams and rivers this is the walk for you: to start Glenmacnass River, swirling and eddying around and over boulders and sand banks. Then Lough Brook, narrower and steeper, chuckling down from Lough Ouler. It is this heart-shaped lake, majestically located below 200m-high cliffs gouged into the shoulder of lofty Tonelagee that is the worthy target of this simple there-and-back walk.

Getting There: By car to *Sally Gap* and thence southward for about 7 miles to Glenmacnass carpark. You can also get there from *Glendalough* by taking the road towards Sally Gap. The total distance from Dublin is about 24 miles.

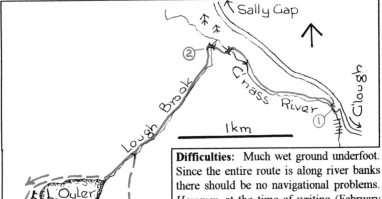

Difficulties: Much wet ground underfoot. Since the entire route is along river banks there should be no navigational problems. *However*, at the time of writing (February 1998), the bridge over Glenmacnass River has been washed away. See if it has been replaced by getting out of the car where forest ends on the right about a mile or so north of Glenmacnass carpark. If it hasn't, you can probably still do the walk by fording the river elsewhere, one point being about 70m upstream of the carpark.

Walking Time: 2 hours (distance 6km, climb 200m) to the lake and return.

Route: ① From the carpark walk upstream along Glenmacnass River, climb two friendly fences and then cross the bridge over the river. Shortly cross a second bridge over a stream (Lough Brook) opposite a forest corner on the far bank of the Glenmacnass. ② Turn left immediately to follow Lough Brook all the way to Lough Ouler. Along here the views gradually open out, rocky Carrigshouk to the right, Knocknacloghoge behind and the cliffs enfolding Lough Ouler ahead.

When you reach the lake you should take an amble around it. More ambitiously, you might like to climb Tonelagee, which should take about 1¼ hours altogether, but please, only if you have a map and compass. If you do so you can return along the south-east shore of the lake.

For both routes return to the carpark by the same route as you ascended.

GLENMALURE

The long, narrow valley of Glenmalure attracts fewer visitors than Glendalough, but it is just as scenic and certainly more rugged. Its steep sides yield tough walks (routes 35, 36). Still, the other walks given here are easier, with little climbing in the case of route 39. Splendid lakes are the targets of two of the routes (35, 38) and a memorable side valley the target of route 36.

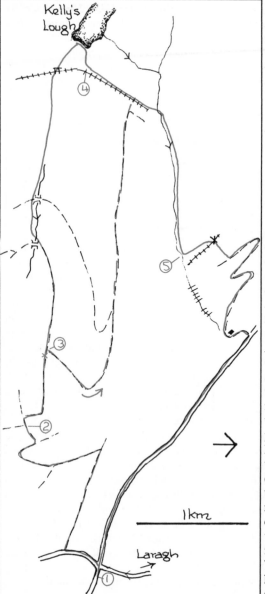

ROUTE 35:
KELLY'S LOUGH

A tough walk. A long trudge upward on forest tracks and a difficult walk to a stream's source leads to a commanding position above Kelly's Lough, a lake wedged in by high mountains on most sides and one of the most remote and lovely spots in Wicklow. The return is initially along a stream and then steeply down into Glenmalure.

Getting There: Car to *Drumgoff Crossroads*, Glenmalure. Turn left here and park immediately in the *private* carpark on the right. The pub opposite would appreciate your patronage after the walk.

Difficulties: Apart from the tough terrain and climbing mentioned above the main route demands a map and compass. If in doubt stick to the easy variation as the navigation is simpler.

Walking Time: 4½ hours (distance 12.5km, climb 500m) for the main route, 4¼ hours (distance 13.5km, climb 480m) for the easy variation. In the former case some time is allowed for rough terrain.

Route: ① Walk back to the crossroads, turn left and, following the Wicklow Way, turn right with it onto a forest track. You can now forget about detailed navigation for some time and concentrate on the climb, steadily upward on the Wicklow Way through mostly felled forest.

② Where the Wicklow Way branches left and starts to drop, continue straight ahead to turn right at the nearby first junction. Pass a forest bar and just beyond it, at another junction right you will have to decide on the main route or the variation. If in doubt choose the variation.

③ For the main route continue straight ahead for about 10 minutes until the track swings left over a major bridge. Turn right off the track here, walking along a stream (the reason for the bridge) between young trees. Shortly cross another track and continue upward, still following the stream.

Here forestry is nearly all behind (and not before time) and rough, heathery ground ahead. Keep walking north-west beyond the source of the stream with the high ground of Carrawaystick on the left, until you come over the crest of the hill and espy Kelly's Lough, several hundred metres long with steep ground close to its left.

Cross a stile over a fence and descend to the lake, where lingering will be difficult to resist, given both the labour of the climb and the splendid setting. That done, walk back to the fence, descending as you do so. ④ Turn left at it to reach the main stream in the valley, Carrawaystick Brook. Cross the stream and walk downstream along it on a rudimentary path. A pleasant walk with mountains on both sides, though the hillside across the stream is marred by a brutal track.

⑤ Where the ground eventually levels off you will see a fence and gate across your path ahead. Turn left to follow the fence across bogland, crossing it at the next gate. Walk directly downhill from the gate to reach a nearby track (indistinct at this point) and turn left onto it.

From here keep to this zig-zag track all the way down. The views on this descent are excellent with the whole length of Glenmalure seemingly at your feet and the mountains south of Glendalough across the narrow valley. At length you will reach a farmhouse on the valley floor and can cross the two rivers beyond it on stepping stones and a bridge. Make sure you do not disturb the residents: keep quiet and leave gates exactly as you found them. When you reach tarmac turn right. Before you start walking the 2km back to the start, have a look at the waterfall descending into Glenmalure from the south. This is Carrawaystick Brook, which you left as a hastening stream on the bogland above. It's hard to believe that it's the same stream.

Easy Variation: This variation has a lot more monotonous forest track, whose saving grace is that it minimises the chance of getting lost.

Turn right where the main route above continues straight ahead. Walk this forest track in a leisurely arc into the valley holding Carrawaystick Brook. At almost the track's end it takes an abrupt right angle turn to the right, so heading directly for the Brook. Leave the track at the turn, walk to the nearby fence, cross it and head upwards following it. After a few minutes leave it to walk west to nearby Kelly's Lough. Follow the main route from here on.

ROUTE 36: FRAUGHAN ROCK GLEN

The Fraughan Rock Glen is a high, gently sloping valley running at right angles to Glenmalure. It is hemmed in longitudinally by fine cliffs and steep slopes and terminated at its higher end by a spectacular set of rapids. The only easy approach to this Shangri-La of the Wicklow mountains is through forest, but once beyond it the rest of the walk, though by no means easy underfoot, is delightful.

Getting There: Drive to *Drumgoff Crossroads*, turn right and continue to the head of the valley about 3½ miles further on to park in the large carpark. The total distance from Dublin is about 40 miles.

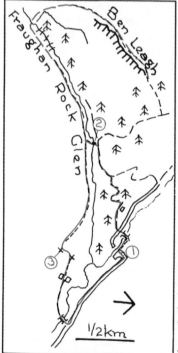

Difficulties: Rough terrain in the Glen itself and one stream to cross which may be difficult after rain; otherwise fairly easy, underfoot and navigationally.

Walking Time: 2 hours (distance 5.5km, climb 200m), so allowing some time for the river crossing and rough ground. The time for the hard variation is 3¼ hours (distance 8km, climb 580m).

Route: ① Walk upstream from the carpark for a few metres to take the footbridge across the river. Cross the tarmac road and plunge into forest on a narrow track on the other side heading diagonally right. At a fine cut-stone ruin on the right, reached in a few minutes, the track definitely opts for path status, and zig-zags upwards, to finally terminate at a forest track. Turn left uphill here. (Incidentally, if you have already decided to return by the same route you should note this point, though even if you miss it the forestry track leads down to the main valley.)

Follow the track to the first junction, where one branch goes straight ahead and the other swings sharply right. ② Don't take either branch: instead cross the river on the left on rudimentary stepping stones. You are now in the heart of the Fraughan Rock Glen, a stern and remote valley with the mighty cliffs of Ben Leagh on the right, a semi-waterfall terminating the valley ahead and the steep shoulder of Clohernagh on the left.

Once across the river, turn right to walk between fence and stream and so avoid private property. You can wander upstream as far as you like into increasingly glorious terrain but perhaps the best place to turn back is around the bottom of the first of three sets of rapids that bound the back of the valley. It's a tough climb after this and the views, though gradually widening, might not justify the effort. However if the day is fine, the time adequate and the lungs and limbs fully functional, you might like to consider the hard variation.

From the rapids return to where you forded the river. This time do not cross it. Instead continue downstream to pick up a rough path obstructed by many boulders. This will lead you into rough country with steeply rising rocky ground on the right and the now formidable stream on the left. ③ After 15 minutes or so from the point where you didn't re-cross the river (hope you don't regret it) you will come to a cross-ways fence with two gates; cross that to the left. Beyond it take an overgrown path to a few deserted farm buildings. Walk the track which starts here to cross a bridge leading onto tarmac. Turn left and walk less than a kilometre back to the start.

Hard Variation: As you advanced up the Fraughan Rock Glen you may have admired the great cliffs of Ben Leagh up to the right and decided that you *must* walk along their tops. If so and if, and only if you know what you are about, climb to the top of the rapids (and the highest point of the block of forest on your right). Walk north along boggy ground using a trace of a path to reach the cliffs where there is a well-developed path. Return by the same route. (Yes, you can walk onward north-east on a path, but it gets increasingly rough, slippery and indistinct before it reaches a track and so cannot be recommended.)

Note

As you walk higher into the Fraughan Rock Glen, you will notice the sudden change in slope in the mountain across Glenmalure behind you. Lower down there is a steep slope, but further up the ground suddenly assumes a much gentler gradient. This is quite a common phenomenon in the east of the Wicklow mountains. The change in slope marks the top of a glacier which gouged its way down the valley from left to right, deepening the former V-shaped lower valley into a U. The reason this feature occurs in the east of the range is because snow tended to accumulate on this, the sheltered side rather than on the more exposed west.

This phenomenon is even better displayed as you walk route 38 below.

ROUTE 37: ABOVE GLENMALURE

A short walk, initially with a lot of climbing from the valley floor of Glenmalure. The views are not all that varying but are predictably good especially down into the narrow glacial valley of Glenmalure and across it to Carrawaystick Waterfall and the mountains of the Lugnaquillia massif.

Getting There: Drive to *Drumgoff Crossroads*, turn right and continue for 2.0 miles to park in the small carpark on the right. The total distance from Dublin is 38 miles.

Difficulties: Easy underfoot. Navigation is another matter. It's a simple matter to wander thoughtlessly along the forest tracks in this area but if you do so you will very soon lose this route. You might consider this to be no great loss but if you really want to walk the route as described here you are going to need an otherwise idle finger to keep on the appropriate point on the map or text, as this is an area with lots of similar decision points. The preoccupation with route finding in the description below is I hope understandable.

Walking Time: 2¼ hours (distance 8km, climb 300m).

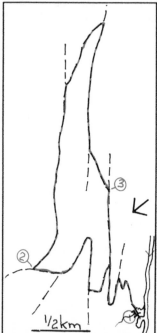

Route: ① From the carpark take the delightful path on the right of the carpark (as you face away from the road). This will take you over a nearby stream and then steeply up to reach a forest track. Take a note of the path at this junction as you might easily miss it on the return. Turn left onto the track to walk round a hairpin bend and at the Wicklow Way marker turn left up a path, so joining the Way, or rather the present (late 1997) route of the Way.

Another steep climb ensues, at the end of which turn right with the Way and then first left to keep on the Way. Fork right at the next junction and now in dense forest, take the next right, so leaving the Way. At this point you are no doubt sick and tired of following directions - so I am glad to tell you that there are no more, for a while anyway.

② The track now meanders across the mountainside without further branches for about 1½km (about 15 minutes) before reaching a fork onto which you turn right downhill. At the next junction turn sharply right, slightly uphill and at the following fork left downhill onto a grassier track, which ends shortly on yet another track, the Wicklow Way again. ③ Turn right onto it and continue straight ahead where the Way heads as a path uphill to the right. You are now on the initial route, so you will know to round the hairpin bend and then look out carefully on the right for the path leading to the carpark where you started.

ROUTE 38: ART'S LOUGH

Sheltered on one long side by steep rocky ground, Art's Lough nestles in the midst of some of the most dramatic country in the mountains. There is only one easy way of getting there (and unfortunately the same easy way of returning). This means a slog up from Glenmalure's valley floor through forestry which mercifully doesn't impede views down into and across Glenmalure.

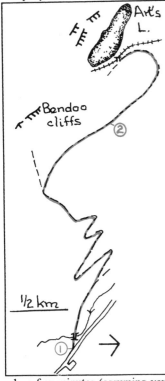

Getting There: Drive to *Drumgoff Crossroads*, turn right and continue for 2.1 miles to park in the forestry entrance on the left. The total distance from Dublin is 38 miles.

Difficulties: Near Art's Lough pay attention to navigation where a section of path trembles on the brink of extinction.

Walking Time: 2½ hours (distance 8km, climb 380m).

Route: ① From the forestry entrance, walk away from the road to cross the nearby bridge and take the track beyond in a series of zig-zags high above the valley floor. There are a few minor tracks off the main one but they don't amount to much and all are cul-de-sacs. At length you will come under the minor cliffs of Bendoo, a good place for a rest before the relentless advance resumes.

② After less than an hour's walking the track comes to an end, but continues as a path, a path of sorts, because it is quite indistinct and in places a high bank on the left is a better indication of the route than the path itself. This worrying stretch lasts only a few minutes (assuming you don't wander into the surrounding heathery slopes, and if you do you will really have problems). Then the path resumes distinctly on a leftward swing through high heather, with a fence on the right. Keep to the path until you shortly meet a stile with the lake beyond.

You will surely be impressed by Art's Lough. Several hundred metres long, it is bounded on its far side by imposing steep, rocky ground and commands magnificent views. There appears to be neither inlet or outlet stream to the lake. Whatever about the inlet, there is in fact an outlet stream. It runs underground from the right end of the lake (right, that is from the viewpoint at the stile) to cascade down into the Fraughan Rock Glen. It is well worthwhile walking to this end of the lake to see the Glen and Ben Leagh cliffs beyond it.

The return should be quite easy, particularly after you have negotiated the anxiety-inducing section near the lake.

ROUTE 39: BALLYBRAID

The small, open valley of Ballybraid lies just off the Military Road north of Glenmalure and offers a diversity of field and farm, moorland, scattered trees and forestry plantations as well as the occasional glimpse of high hills. An easy and pleasant walk though with some difficult ground underfoot.

Getting There: Drive to *Laragh*, here fork left onto the R755. After less than a mile fork right (signposted 'Glenmalure'), drive to the crest of the hill, pass the Shay Elliot memorial on the left and park at the next junction on the right (it slants acutely back). The total distance from Dublin is about 35 miles.

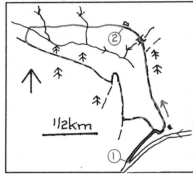

Difficulties: Much mud underfoot. Navigation is easy except at one point noted below, but an error here should not prove hazardous.

Walking Time: 1½ hours (distance 4.5km, climb 120m).

Route: ① Take the dirt road from the junction, forking shortly right to pass a fine stone-built house on the right. Here the road, rough up to this, definitely attains track status, and heads gently upward with the lower fields of Ballybraid down on the left. Ignore minor tracks on the right to pass several houses, which look deserted, but may not be, so exercise caution.

At the last house in the valley, which is set parallel to the track and on its right you will clearly see the terrain ahead. At your feet, fields and beyond them rough moorland, to the right the rising flank of Cullentragh, and on the left a mature forestry plantation, the latter of more than academic interest, as a track in it provides the return route.

② From this last house therefore, head onward through the fields keeping to a grassy, almost notional track roughly contouring across the slope. This course will take you over one stream, and to a second, a much more formidable affair, cutting diagonally through the moorland. From the banks of this stream you should be able to see the return track up to the left in the forest; the problem being to reach it. To do so cross the stream and walk no more than about a hundred metres along the forest edge, seeking an easy way across the main stream in the valley and then up through the trees. There is a path running directly upward, but curiously it is clearer away from the bank so don't worry too much if you don't find it.

Once on the forest track, troubles are behind. Turn left onto it, turn left at the next junction to swing immediately round a hairpin bend, take the next turn on the left and turn right close to the substantial house passed earlier. The start is a short distance away.